One Journey:
7 Ships

The 7 Ships Needed to Navigate the Waters of Life

Nahchon D. Guyton

One Journey: 7 Ships. Copyright © 2019. Nahchon D. Guyton. All rights reserved.

No part of this book may be reproduced, stored in a retrieval system, or transmitted in any form or by any means, electronic, mechanical, photocopying, recording or otherwise, without prior permission of the author.

PUBLISHED BY:

www.hcpbookpublishing.com

ISBN: 978-1-949343-29-8 (PAPERBACK)

ISBN: 978-1-949343-30-4 (EBOOK)

Scripture taken from the New King James Version®. Copyright © 1982 by Thomas Nelson. Used by permission. All rights reserved.

For more information on Nahchon D. Guyton, visit www.nahchon.com and feel free to leave your comments and opinions about this book and your personal journey.

There is more to life than what you have experienced. Take this journey and experience more.

"Life is too short to live in fear, and too long to live with regrets; so, do something great. You only have one life to live, so live it well."

~ Nahchon D. Guyton ~

Table of Contents

Dedications 12
Preface 14
    Ministry of Christ 18
    He Understood That He Had a Purpose 19
    Today, I Choose 19
Introduction 21
    Why Did I Write This Book? 21
    Act Now: Time Is Limited 22
    Confession To Stay Pliable 22
    You Can Refuse The Gift 23
    My Will At Work 23
    We Are Never Waiting On Him 23
    We Can Accomplish More 24
    We All Have Greatness Within Us 24
    Never Too Old to Start 25
Foundation For The 7 Ships: Understanding 26
    In All Communication, There Is Noise 27
    Noise Will And Does Cause Confusion 27
    We Have To Talk 28
    Opportunity To Learn 29
    7 Ships Needed To Navigate The Waters Of Life 29
    Definitions Of The 7 Ships 30
    Jesus, Born Into The World 31
    Jesus Was Abraham's Legacy 32
    God The Father, Coming In The Flesh As Jesus 32

The Purpose For Jesus 32
What Does God Require Of Us? 33
He Gave Us Free Will 34
Our Design... 34
The Innocent Paid It All For The Guilty 35
We Cannot Save Or Redeem Anyone 36
The Exchange: Life For Death 37
God Is Love 37
The Goal 38

CHAPTER 1: Explanation Of The Journey 43
Why Should We Have A Personal Relationship? 44
Time... 45
Time Does Not Differ For Anyone 46
The Story Of Two Wolves 47
Learn How To Feed The Spirit.. 48
A Custom Life For Each Of Us 48
Understanding Is A Form Of Protection 49
One Step At A Time 50
The Elusive "It"... 50
"It" Has Been Discovered Over 2000 Years Ago 51
The Promise Fulfilled 52
Diamonds From Heaven.. 52
Humble Yourself 53
Battlefields Of Life.. 54
Chapter 1 Outro 56
Chapter 1 Take Away 56

CHAPTER 2: Relationship: The One Who Should Matter The Most... 59
The First Relationship 59
A Better Plan For Us 60
Relationship With God.. 61

    God Dropped Jesus 62
    Define Relationships 64
    Who Are They? 65
    See Him As He Is 65
    Goal Of The Relationship 66
    Beauty For Ashes 66
    The Person On The Street 67
    Always Desire To Give 69
    Leave Me Alone 70
    Now, It Is Our Turn To Give 71
    Close To The Father 73
    Chapter 2 Outro 75
    Chapter 2 Take Away 75

CHAPTER 3: What Is True Fellowship? 77
    Eat While You Negotiate 78
    A Meal Together: Fellowship 81
    FELLOWSHIP: Short Definition: Common, Shared, And Unclean
    84
    Life 86
    Call On Him In The Storm 87
    Prayer To Accept Christ 88
    Chapter 3 Outro 90
    Chapter 2 Take Away 90

Chapter 4: The Power of Real Friendship 93
    To Be A Friend 94
    Friendships Are Often Tested 96
    A Praiseworthy Friend 97
    To The Cross 99
    The Most Important Person In The Room 100
    Godly Friendships 101
    The Move 102

Chapter 4 Outro 105
Chapter 4 Take Away 106

CHAPTER 5: Discipleship: Learning From the Master 107

Following Comes At A Price 108
Become Like The Teacher.. 109
Modern Discipleship 110
Export What We Grow... 112
Choices Just Are 113
Choices And Decisions Are Not The Same 114
Balance In Everything 115
We Must Be Disciplined 116
Follow Christ From Our Hearts...................................... 117
Life Will Provide Opportunities For Change 118
Challenge All Your Thoughts 119
Think Of The Mind As A Radio...................................... 121
Tend To Your Forest Daily 122
What We Say Does Matter 124
The Art of the Tongue 126
Speak With Purpose 127
Your Words, Your Sword.. 129
Words 130
Speech From One Generation To The Next 131
Master Your Thoughts... 132
God Given Seeds 134
We Are In A Battle 136
Become One With Your Two 139
Stop Pretending 140
Prayer... 141
Chapter 5 Outro 141
Chapter 5 Take Away 142

Chapter 6: Stewardship: Managing Our Resources 143
    Stewardship Over All 146
    What House Has Your Heart? What Car Drives You? 148
    Love Is The Investment 149
    Give Your Best 149
    Selfishness And Not Selflessness 150
    Share It And Make It Grow 151
    Jesus Was And Is Our Example 153
    God Is Looking For A Faithful Servant 153
    Chapter 6 Outro 155
    Chapter 6 Take Away 155

CHAPTER 7: Partnership: Collaborating With God The Father Through Jesus And Others 157
    Connecting With The Right Partners 158
    We Suffer From The Lack Of A Real Connection 160
    God Wants Us To Collaborate With Him 161
    The Enemy Of Progress Is Stagnation 162
    Ask Questions 163
    The Difference With Jesus 165
    An Effective Partner 166
    Chapter 7 Outro 168
    Chapter 7 Take Away 168

CHAPTER 8: Leadership: Learning To Follow, So We Can Lead 171
    GPS Defined 172
    Because People Follow Them, Doesn't Make Them A Leader .. 173
    Why Were They Able To Achieve Such Greatness? 174
    Story Of A Good King 177
    Before It All, He Was 177
    What Have You Been Saying? 179
    Modern Leader 180

Self-Perception 180
A Good Leader 182
To Lead Is A Gift 183
Experience Trumps Theory Everytime 185
How Are You At Following? 185
Opportunity To Demonstrate Leadership 187
Heart of a Good Leader 188
Traits Of A Leader 190
Desire To Serve 193
Chapter 8 Outro 195
Chapter 8 Take Away 195

CHAPTER 9: Who Am I? The Age-Old Question 197

Who Am I? 197
Real Power Versus Perceived 198
Beyond The Passive And Into The Active 199
The Race For Life 201
Moral Of The Story 207
Closing Remarks 208

APPENDIX: Question And Answers 213
Types Of Love From The Greek 215
Love 218
Fruits Of The Flesh 221
Fruits Of The Flesh Defined 221
Fruits Of The Spirit 227
Fruits Of The Spirit Defined 227

Dedications

First, I must give honor and thanks to Jesus, my Lord and Savior.

This book is dedicated to my life partner and wife, Crystal; my daughter, Christchon; my son, Tristan, and to the people who inspired me throughout this journey called my life.

Special thanks and gratitude to my grandmothers, Rosemary Guyton, and Chestina Ezell-McCarthy, who have gone home to be with the Lord.

I want to thank my mother, Ruth Hemingway; my father, Russell Guyton, and my second mom, Caroline Guyton. You all helped me to finish this book.

To those I did not mention because there are far too many to list, please know that I appreciate you just as much.

I hope that wherever this book finds you, that the message, the spirit and the concepts that grace these pages will bless you on your journey.

Nothing is more important than knowing our Lord and Savior Jesus Christ, so I hope through the reading of this book that you get a good introduction to Him and understand that He loves you.

Preface

Life is a journey that requires our participation, if we want to succeed and live an abundant life. Success is not a measure of what you gain only, but rather a process of pouring out and into others. Making a difference in the life of someone else, being the hope for another, and learning along the way is the path to success. Life is a team sport; you need a team to do life well.

The purpose of our journey is to make us aware of our custom path that leads to success, and to teach us how to endure the process without shortcuts. A shortcut is something we take to avoid going through the storms and/or the process. Learning as we go through the storms of life and going through the process is how we learn endurance. If we want to live a life of abundance, we must understand that avoiding issues is not the way to success.

Spend time in the process learning and growing. The trials and tribulations of life, whatever they may be, can awakened us to the still calm voice of God. When we are in pain, or facing a difficult circumstance, we have the largest opportunity to gain understanding for an abundant life. The changes, trials and the state of being uncomfortable is where we uncover the gems of success which are locked in the tribulations of our personal journey. To speed up the process is to learn to listen and lean on that still small voice that guides us all. That still small voice is the voice of God.

We should focus on building a real relationship with God the Father and learn what He has put in us for the benefit of the world and our success on Earth. We are all here to live an abundant life with Him as the head. The journey is where we learn what it means to be alive.

The journey called life is not simply getting things, doing what you want and going where you please. The journey is about learning, growing and flourishing in your understanding of God and this gift of life. We are His investment, and, like any great investment, He expects a positive return.

We will gain the most through the process of change. We all should seek to learn from the trials we go through, and not be so focused on the results than the lessons. Results are critical to lasting success and extremely important, but not as important as learning the lessons. If I point out a street sign to you, you must first be able to see the sign, and comprehend what it means in order to benefit from it. If you do not see the street sign, you will not be able to benefit from the knowledge the sign contains. This is true for all processes and challenges. If we don't see the value in the lesson, we will not be able to benefit from the process.

We do not learn at the end of a process but during the process. Similar to an exam, the results show us what we learned or did not learn from the process. We will become the person He designed us to be, only if we learn how to be present, thankful and appreciate the process. *What did we learn?* No matter what we go through, we must learn to be thankful for our team (family, friends, partners and mentors).

The process are the trials, tribulations, and the challenges of life. The process is often uncomfortable. Change is constant, and most people hate change because they fear the unknown. Change is the only way to grow and progress. We all know people who have been going through the same issues for years, some of them may be us. If we do not change, we will continue to go through changes, difficulties, challenges and upheavals because we refuse to learn and change our minds and hearts. We will continue to go through those issues until we learn the lessons. We must learn quickly because our legacy depends on it.

Legacy; the marks, impact, and difference we leave behind, will be the results of what we have learned while on the journey. If we believe that the destination is the goal, then we are missing the point of the process and the journey.

Dr. Martin Luther King Jr. was assassinated on April 4, 1968. His death was tragic, but his death was not his legacy. What he did while he was living is what we celebrate. We celebrate the way he overcame the trials, tribulations and challenges of the day, to make it better for them that followed; that is legacy. He did his best then, so we could live a better life now.

Let us look at Jesus' journey to the cross. If the cross was the destination, we would miss the beauty of the ministry of Jesus and the Gospel. He died on the cross, but I like to reason that the cross was not the goal. The goal was redemption, reconciliation and spreading God's love. The cross was just a part of the process.

What He did in the last three years of His life on earth is what the gospel is built on. *Why celebrate His death?* His life is what mattered then and now. He died on the cross but rose again to make a point to all who followed Him that death has no power over Him or us for that matter. We are eternal beings who will never really die. We will live forever, but our time on this Earth is limited, so we must make the most of our time here. We must live in such a way now that our legacy will live on.

As we journey on in this life, we too will have a cross to bear. It is a part of the process. We must hold on to our faith knowing that this too will pass, if we are willing to endure to the end.

MINISTRY OF CHRIST

As we consider the ministry of Christ, notice I did not say the ministry of Jesus. I would like to point out that even though Jesus and the Christ are the same, they are two different people contained in one vessel. They are one body, with one soul and yet they are two, which became one.

To learn and grow in any form, we must participate in the process of study and learning. Active participation requires awareness, attention to the fact that something of significance is happening. Think of it like this, we must be present in mind and in the moment. Our attention and participation are required for us to grow through the process.

HE UNDERSTOOD THAT HE HAD A PURPOSE

Jesus understood His purpose so much that He told His parents that He was about His Father's business. He was 12 years old. He understood that He had a purpose and that He had to participate in the process to fulfill His purpose. Jesus was not going to let His situation dictate His purpose. *Are you as clear on your purpose as Jesus was at 12 years old?* Jesus had a definite purpose, and an inner knowing about who He was and why He was here. Let us examine His journey to improve our own.

Let us take this journey together, making the choice to learn, grow and develop according to God's purpose so we can be all we were created to be in Christ Jesus. You can start by making these your daily declarations:

TODAY, I CHOOSE

Today, I choose to be great.

Today, I refuse to settle for anything less than my all.

Today, I will give 100 percent of my mind and effort.

Today, I will stand for something.

Today, I will stand up for someone, even if it is just in truth.

Today, I will be king of my destiny.

Today, I refuse to allow life's circumstances to dictate my faith. I will show my faith by my commitment to self and the communities where I live and work.

Today, I will learn something new.

Today, I will do something new.

Today, I will teach someone.

Today, I will share myself, and knowledge with others.

Today, I will be true to self and all those I encounter.

Today, I will live my life with honesty, integrity, and self-respect.

Today, I choose to be happy.

Today, I will be all that I can be, because today is all I have.

Introduction

WHY DID I WRITE THIS BOOK?

I wrote this book for several reasons, the main reason being that God told me to write it. I know it was the Lord because He was clear and patient as He led me to the Scriptures that support the concepts He wanted me to write. When the Lord asked me to write this book, I was just coming out of being unemployed but sustained by His grace for almost a year. I was just catching my breath from being unemployed, and I was not in a writing mood. Even though I am a creative writer, poet, motivational writer, and business/program writer, and I always wanted to write a book, that was not the time I had in mind. The Father said otherwise, so I wrote what He gave. I am not a trained writer nor an English major. My major is information technology, graphic design and web development so if I was to write anything, it should have been about building, repairing and operating computers, or creating web pages or a logo.

Nonetheless, God wanted me to write about these 7 Ships: (***Relationship, Friendship, Fellowship, Discipleship, Stewardship, Partnership and Leadership***) and share how they affect and ultimately shape our lives.

ACT NOW; TIME IS LIMITED

Most people shy away from their purpose as if they are the source. We feel inadequate, incapable of pulling off the request alone, as if God has chosen the wrong person. Some go as far as making excuses for why they cannot obey the request. They give one reason after another as to why God must be wrong for picking them to do what He asked. We should never allow fear to keep us from accepting the offer of being God's hands and feet in the world.

Many are afraid, just like I was, that they do not have what it takes to finish. We are not the source but the vessel. God is the artist and we are the clay. He molds, shapes and builds what He desires, and all we need to do is yield to the process.

CONFESSION TO STAY PLIABLE

I have prayed and confessed to my team (family, friends and mentors) on several occasions that I want to die empty. With every drop of good, and fruitful knowledge that God has given me, I knew I could only write this book with Jesus as my Lord and Savior and the Holy Spirit as my guide.

All good gifts come from the Father above. God gave me this book, not for me to hold it for myself, but to share it with you and the world.

What has God giving you to share?

You Can Refuse the Gift

We have the power to say no to Him, His gift of eternal life, and His ways because He gave us free will. He bought us with a price; Jesus' life. We can say no to the gift, but why not say yes to His offer of eternity with Him as head of our life?

I accepted the gift of Jesus and let Him be Lord and savior of my life. By accepting the gift, I gave up my rights to a life that I deserved, for a life I could not earn in a thousand life times; eternal life. I gained access to eternal life because I surrendered my will to His.

My Will at Work

Years ago, I tried to write another book and it turned out to be more of a training guide or workbook than a book. Yes, that was my will at work. I was writing but God was not inspiring or guiding me. When I was trying to write, it was a lot harder than it should have been, and it required more effort. Writing a book is not an easy task for anyone.

We Are Never Waiting On Him

Whenever I sat down to write this book, the Lord provided the words. It may have come together sooner if I had not wasted writing time doing other things. God is always waiting on us to get out of our own way, so He can have His way and take us from glory to glory or, in my own words, from greatness to greatness. God is always moving on our behalf and waiting for us to get out of the way. We often foul up and destroy some of the simplest tasks set before us because we are not paying attention to the process or listening to the Father's instructions via the Holy Spirit.

We Can Accomplish More

We can accomplish more if we stop being so reluctant to step out in faith and do what God has called us to do. Many people will die with the solutions the world needs. They have answers to problems hidden deep within them; answers to cancer, traffic and social ills, etc., but it never manifests because of fear. The same amount of energy it takes to believe in fear is the same required to act in faith.

We All Have Greatness Within Us

We all have greatness within us. God created us that way, but we can only access it fully by allowing Jesus to expose us to the open doors. Jesus is the key to us walking in our greatness. I am not talking about the Jesus of religion, but the Jesus that you will come to know and discover through a real, honest relationship. Jesus wants you to live life to its fullest, in abundance of faith and truth.

NEVER TOO OLD TO START

You are never too old to start the journey. Take the necessary steps today to be a better you. The world is waiting on what you will bring to make it a better place for the next generation. Suspend your desire to be right in your own eyes. Take God's mercy and trust His grace. Allow Him to shape and mold you into the person He created you to be. Let Him provide for your needs, wants, and the desires of your heart.

Foundation For The 7 Ships: Understanding

IN ALL COMMUNICATION, THERE IS NOISE

Most people are not usually speaking the same language, even though they are using the same words, terms, and sometimes the same dialect. Most people in North America speak English as their primary language. Others may speak multiple languages and English is their second language. Same language, different meaning. Now imagine you were speaking to someone from the South and you are from the North East. You want to go get some fresh produce, so you ask for the nearest bodega. The other person looks at you with utter confusion. The odds are, they have no idea what you mean.

NOISE WILL AND DOES CAUSE CONFUSION

As the speaker, we take it for granted that we are being clear. We know what we mean when we speak, but in all communication, there is noise. Noise will and does cause confusion to the receiver. Most of us speak with little concern about the noise. We just spout off what we want to relay, then we are upset when we are misunderstood.

There are a variety of factors that come to play in the confusion; culture, emotions, climate of the space, inflection, tone and body language. The listener or receiver is interrupting the message through their lens, not ours, and that is why we end up in confusion.

Noise is anything that can and does hinder clear transmitting and receiving of a message.

WE HAVE TO TALK

When a woman tells a man, "We have to talk", consider those same words but with two totally different interpretations of the meaning and intent.

To limit the noise that is always present in communication, we must purposefully define the words used and clarify what we want the listener to understand in the exchange. This can be accomplished by asking questions, for example, *"What did you hear when I said this?"* Or ask them to explain what they understood. Listening, learning and communicating all require active participation on the part of the listener and the sender.

With that said, as we journey, I hope to have your full attention as we dive into exploring the 7 Ships (**Relationship, Friendship, Fellowship, Discipleship, Stewardship, Partnership and Leadership**) that influence all our lives.

OPPORTUNITY TO LEARN

My hope is that we learn something new about ourselves or at least get a revelation about ourselves and God from these 7 Ships. We often think we understand what a word or phrase means and in doing so, we remove the opportunity to learn what the speaker meant by a particular word or phrase. This could be a grave mistake in some cases, but in most cases, it adds to the noise and can accelerate the breakdown in communication.

7 SHIPS NEEDED TO NAVIGATE THE WATERS OF LIFE

Here are the 7 Ships: ***Relationship, Friendship, Fellowship, Discipleship, Stewardship, Partnership and Leadership.*** We use these 7 Ships to navigate the waters of life. We are going to explore these 7 Ships in Jesus's life to illustrate Jesus' redeeming love for all humanity. We will compare how the world uses them and focus on and looking to Holy Spirit for a greater insight into what they mean to us, and for us, on a personal and spiritual level.

The goal is to help you understand these 7 Ships. We approach this with openness, making room for the Holy Spirit to show the way, thus producing a greater return. We only know in part. In order to know more, we need the Holy Spirit to reveal and guide us to the solutions, opportunities and wisdom.

DEFINITIONS OF THE 7 SHIPS

Fellowship: *a member of a group having common characteristics, goals and worldview, known to share the challenges of life with nothing hidden, often over a meal.*

Relationship: *connecting or binding participants in a relationship, where both parties benefit from the union, but not always equally.*

Friendship: *one attached to another by affection or esteem, sharing their best to make sure the other is well; someone to lean on in time of change; someone with whom you share a life, nothing hidden, all is exposed.*

Discipleship: *one who accepts and assists in spreading the doctrines of another, to the point that they adopt the mind of the teacher, speaking in the same manner as the teacher.*

Stewardship: *one who actively directs affairs for themselves or another for the benefit of the owner or themselves; a good manager.*

Partnership: *person with whom one shares an intimate relationship, with the sole purpose to build, create or produce something of value so that both parties can benefit from the proceeds.*

Leadership: *providing direction or guidance through giving of one's time, mind and energy to ensure that the follower is well cared for so they can develop fully, lacking nothing, sometimes* *to the discomfort of the leader, for example, Jesus or a good parent.*

JESUS, BORN INTO THE WORLD

Many have heard of the miracle; the virgin birth of Christ. If not, here it is in short:

> *Now the birth of Jesus Christ was as follows: After His mother Mary was betrothed to Joseph, before they came together, she was found with child of the Holy Spirit. Then Joseph her husband, being a just man, and not wanting to make her a public example, was minded to put her away secretly. But while he thought about these things, behold, an angel of the Lord appeared to him in a dream, saying, "Joseph, son of David, do not be afraid to take to you Mary your wife, for that which is conceived in her is of the Holy Spirit. And she will bring forth a Son, and you shall call His name Jesus, for He will save His people from their sins." (Matthew 1:18-21)*
>
> *And she brought forth her firstborn Son, and wrapped Him in swaddling cloths, and laid Him in a manger, because there was no room for them in the inn. (Luke 2:7)*

JESUS WAS ABRAHAM'S LEGACY

I want to offer you a different take on the story using the 7 Ships as the basis for my perspective. Jesus was born a relative to Abraham by virtue of His relationship with Joseph, His earthly father. Jesus was Abraham's legacy. He was a direct descendant of Abraham through the process of adoption. Jesus became a descendant of Abraham by way of his adopted father, Joseph. (*See Matthew 1:1–17 for the full lineage of Jesus*)

Why is this important? Abraham, known as a friend of God, walked with God, and believed God. (*See James 2:23*)

GOD THE FATHER, COMING IN THE FLESH AS JESUS

What was the purpose for God to come to Earth as Jesus? Adam's fall through disobedience caused all humanity to disconnect from God. There was no one else who was blameless and without sin that could redeem man, so God gave us His only begotten Son so we could have a chance to get back to our rightful place with God the Father. From the beginning, God wanted to fellowship with us, as our leader, and friend. We are His partners in caring for the earth. (*See Genesis 2*)

THE PURPOSE FOR JESUS

God wanted a direct connection to us without any outside interference. God did not want lawgivers, or rule-setters such as the Priest, Pastor or Rabbi coming between Him and us. God can use them to build and share the gospel, but He did not want our relationship with Him to be filtered through men. He wanted to be our all, our friend, our leader, our partner, our savior, and our God. God knew that He needed to show us by example how to live a sinless life in Jesus. God is a just God, so someone had to pay the debt for our sin.

What Does God Require Of Us?

God was planning to do all the heavy lifting. All He requires of us is love and obedience, to become a disciple who would seek fellowship with Him daily and be a good steward over all He provided. He wants us as a friend, but not the kind of friend we find in today's world. He wants a true friend who sticks closer than a brother. You will find this definition of friendship used throughout this book. God desires to be an intricate part of our lives, because He has a deep affection for us. God desires our friendship and for us to choose Him as King.

Friendship: one attached to another by affection or esteem, sharing their best to make sure the other is well; someone to lean on in time of change; someone with whom you share a life, nothing hidden, all is exposed.

HE GAVE US FREE WILL

The beauty about this life and God's love for us is that we have free will. We can choose to be with God or not. Regardless of our choice, His love never fades. To follow Him or not is our choice. God will never force us to do anything. The difference for most is the amount of pain we suffer trying to navigate the waters of life without Him at the helm; we could forever be separated from Him. God's love is everlasting, but we can close the door on it by not allowing Him in. We can spend eternity in darkness because we refused to accept the gift of light, which comes through a real relationship with God the Father by Jesus Christ.

In the beginning, before the fall, God's goal was to have a relationship with us that would ultimately lead us into a deep friendship, followed by eternal discipleship. He wanted us to take part in the Kingdom of Heaven. He wanted us, as humans, to reign on Earth with Him as King and Lord over all creation, "On earth as it is in heaven." (See Matthew 6:10).

OUR DESIGN

As we explore Christ's journey to and off the cross, we will see what God truly intended for humanity.

Due to our lack of knowledge and understanding of spiritual things, we have become world thinkers, five sense seekers and not world changers. We have become a light of the world and not the light in the world. We believe the lies of the world; that we are limited to the things of this world. Heaven is the Kingdom and God is the King, and we are His children. We can do what our Father says and not what we learned from living in a falling world.

The ground on which we plant our feet is to be sovereign territory. We take it for the King, not by force, but with love and kindness, just as God in Heaven is sovereign and is love. We are not held by the limitations of this world, but we are to demonstrate the love of the Father to the world.

THE INNOCENT PAID IT ALL FOR THE GUILTY

Heaven is not the reward, but I offer the view that it is the training ground where we learn the ways of the Father.

We read in the Bible that at the end of time there will be a new heaven and a new Earth. *(See Revelations 21)*. Why would we need a new Earth, if Heaven were the goal or the reward? We will reign with Jesus for a thousand years on this Earth *(See Revelation 20:6),* then this earth will pass away, and a new heaven and a new earth will come down, and Jesus will be King. That is the way God, the Father, intended from the beginning with Jesus being the King, and us in direct connection with Him for eternity as sons and daughters.

WE CANNOT SAVE OR REDEEM ANYONE

When Jesus returns, He is coming back for His bride; those who took the journey of walking with Him and being a light in the world as a reflection of the redeeming power of the cross. God is not coming to save our flesh. The flesh can never please God. He is coming for our souls. Our souls are comprised of our mind, our will, and our emotions. He wants to redeem our soul and in the process of our redemption, He is asking us to help redeem others by displaying His love to our fellow man. Despite our attempts, we cannot save or redeem anyone. I repeat, we cannot save or redeem the soul of anyone. We can only point them to the One who can save and redeem them; Jesus the Christ.

We are required to point others to Jesus with love and kindness. Jesus did not come to punish, but to save. He came that we might have life and have it more abundantly. I believe it is the Lord's will that we live a full life, not a life of despair, fear, shame, and guilt.

> *These things I have spoken to you, that in Me you may have peace. In the world you will have tribulation; but be of good cheer, I have overcome the world. (John 16:33).*

The good news is that Jesus overcame the world with all its trouble, sin, shame and death. We are in the world, but it does not have rule over us. We have rule over it through Christ Jesus.

The Exchange; Life For Death

Jesus volunteered and took what we deserved by taking the punishment of the cross, so we could share in what He deserved, everlasting life. The journey that we take as followers of Christ requires us to pray for our enemies, and to show our haters the love of Christ. I accept this to be true. We should be willing to take abuse and mistreatment for Christ sake. When it comes to spreading the Good News and the redeeming power of the cross and showing Jesus Christ orchestrating/cultivating good fruit in our lives, we should take whatever comes with that as the Holy Spirit leads us. Salt provides flavor, light brings illumination to dark places, and servants serve by providing for and taking care of others.

Nowhere in that mandate does it call for us to abuse or allow abuse to ourselves by others. This is very important, because Jesus showed kindness to everyone, including the very ones who killed Him.

Through Christ Jesus who strengthens us, we can lean on and lean into the saving arms of our Lord Jesus Christ, and rely on the Holy Spirit to lead, guide, and correct our every step as we journey through life.

God Is Love

Now let us stop and consider what it means when we hear that God is Love. The Scriptures does not say God is made up of love, but God is love. This thing called love embodies His whole existence. Our heavenly Father created us in His likeness and image, so our makeup is love. The same is true for God who is Love. Jesus tells us that if we see Him, we have seen the Father" (*See John 14:9*). Jesus is love too, since He is the full embodiment of the father. (*See Q/A at the end of this book.*)

THE GOAL

The goal of this book is to help you develop a true personal relationship and understanding of who the Father is and how to grow closer to Him through Jesus Christ. If you can apply the truth of the 7 Ships as Jesus did, then I can assure you that you will be prepared to take this journey and live an abundant life.

We will take a closer look at the 7 Ships that Jesus used to redeem us from sin and shame, along with how we too can benefit from these 7 Ships. Jesus did not die and rise again to show us that He was God nor that it was impossible for us, but rather to show God's love for us. He wanted us to know that in God there are no limits to what is possible, but without God, there are all sorts of limitations and impossibilities.

We will begin at the end and walk backwards through time and space to show you the 7 Ships that Jesus used throughout history to shed light on what I feel has been a gross misrepresentation of God and Jesus. The purpose is to help you become a better steward, leader, partner, disciple, and friend who can walk in relationship with God through fellowship with Jesus and other believers.

I would ask that you open your mind and heart to hear what the Spirit is saying as we take this trip of "One Journey: 7 Ships."

The 7 Ships

Let's Begin

CHAPTER 1

Explanation of the Journey

"Dance. Smile. Giggle. Marvel. TRUST. HOPE. LOVE. WISH. BELIEVE. Most of all, enjoy every moment of the journey, and appreciate where you are at this moment instead of always focusing on how far you have to go."

— *Mandy Hale, Author of 'The Single Woman: Life, Love, and a Dash of Sass.'*

Let's begin, *"In the beginning was the Word, and the Word was with God, and the Word was God." (John 1:1).* I want to spend some time here as we talk about the first ship briefly; **Relationship.**

Remember our definition of Relationship: *connecting or binding participants in a relationship, where both parties benefit from the union, but not always equally.*

WHY SHOULD WE HAVE A PERSONAL RELATIONSHIP?

Why should we have a personal relationship with the Father, through is only begotten Son, Jesus Christ? He wants to be a part of our daily lives, or better stated, our eternal life. He never wanted to be a second or third thought; He desires to be the first thought. He desires to speak into each moment. He desires to help us navigate our vessel of life, so that we can fulfill not only His purpose but enjoy some of the gems (the beauty of living) of the journey along the way. Life will not always be full of roses and warm fuzzes all the time. Sometimes you will encounter some harsh relatives, friends and strangers who will seek to destroy you.

Life is a journey so prepare and take it one step at a time and trust the Author and not the story.

You are here to show the world the love of God. You cannot do this if you are not in a true relationship with Him. A true relationship requires a commodity that is limited and often neglected; time.

Time

I am essential to every aspect of life.

I can be your best friend or your worst enemy.

I grow with you or slowly diminish depending on you.

I appear to be forever when you are born; I seem like yesterday as you go on.

I am the measure to which all life is measured.

I am a moment.

Most feel I am forever, when their young and others say I am not enough, when the years have come and gone.

I am to be cherished and utilized, but so often, I am wasted and poorly spent.

I hold the treasures of life and all its pain; what you get depends on you.

I walk with the wealthy and with the poor, the eager and the lazy.

I give freely to him who desires my richness and take from him who would use me for wasted moments and fruitless fun.

I profit the wise and punish the fool.

I am a weapon for life, to be mastered and controlled, so many handle me carelessly.

They blame me for being so little and not all I should be; I give everyone the same portions, so why blame me?

Remember what I said, "I can be your best friend or your worst enemy and it all depends on you."

When I am positioned for battle correctly, I never seem to run short, but let the master hand me over so freely to the world of not and see me vanish right before your eyes.

I will do it smoothly, stealth like, in that moment of realization, I am gone, and you are left surprised.

I am all you have, and you never know when I may decide to leave, so put me to work for your good or wake when I am far spent, and you wish you could.

I am here now, use me. When I am gone, I am gone.

What I yield to you depends on you.

TIME DOES NOT DIFFER FOR ANYONE

Time does not differ for anyone; God wants to know that He is a priority, but not because He is needy or because He needs our time. He wants to spend time with us, so He can help to guide us. He knows what lies behind every choice we may or may not make. He knows the heart of every man, and He understands the heaviness of living on this side. He knows when we grow in our spirit we will no longer be conformed to the leading of the flesh. Where you choose to spend your time is an indication of what you value. All relationships require time. If you have a failing relationship, check the amount of quality time you commit to building, growing and developing that relationship. Relationships are not hard, they can be challenging, and they all require a time commitment.

THE STORY OF TWO WOLVES

The following is a story about two wolves to illustrate the internal war we all fight. Who wins, is up to us.

A grandfather is talking with his grandson and he says there are two wolves inside of us, which are always at war with each other. One of them is a spirit wolf, which represents things like kindness, bravery, and love. The other is a flesh wolf, which represents things like greed, hatred, and fear. The grandson stops and thinks about it for a second, then he looks up at his grandfather and says, "Grandfather, which one wins?" The grandfather quietly replies, "The one you feed."

LEARN HOW TO FEED THE SPIRIT

As the above story illustrates, the one you feed the most is the one that will grow. The one that gets the most time in your heart and mind is the one that will grow. As long as the earth remains, there will be hot and cold, summer, winter, seedtime and harvest (See Genesis 8:22). Once you plant the seed, you have to give it some time if you expect to see the harvest. Do not think that you are wasting time by cultivating relationships with people of God. I am not talking about people who attend church out of duty, but people who know the Father in spirit and truth because they have a relationship with Him. You will know them when you see them.

A CUSTOM LIFE FOR EACH OF US

Consider for a moment that I am hiring you to build me a custom home. Would you not seek me for instructions as it relates to my wants, likes, dislikes preferences and desires so you could build according to my vision? God is seeking this kind of consideration. He designed a custom life for each of us. In order to live that custom life, we have to seek the One who designed it. This requires that we spend time with Him and His people. We were created to be in relationship with God and His people. Spending time with God and His people gives us understanding of who He is, who we are and how God works in our lives.

UNDERSTANDING IS A FORM OF PROTECTION

Have you ever been in a conversation with someone and even though both of you were speaking English, you had little to no idea of what they were trying to tell you?

Understanding is defined as *information that a person can stand under.* When you truly understand something, it covers you. When you understand your rights as a citizen of a country, and you visit another country, you stand under the citizenship and protection of your homeland. Understanding is a form of protection. It covers us in a variety of ways, and that is why we can stand under that information.

King Solomon wrote:

> *Wisdom is the principal thing; therefore get wisdom. And in all your getting, get understanding. (Proverbs 4:7).*

We could avoid a lot of pain if we sought to get a full understanding of matters. Most of us would rather just jump into something with little or no understanding, then we get hurt and want to blame everyone but the guilty one, ourselves. We need to seek to understand God and His ways if we want to have a successful Journey.

ONE STEP AT A TIME

Every journey starts the same; one-step at a time in a direction with the hope of finding it, whatever it may be. We are looking for the next great thing, the last tribe in the rain forest, or some hidden treasure in the middle of nowhere. We are looking for something, and sometimes we are in search of ourselves.

Often, we are not willing to stop the search until we have uncovered it. It is what drives our search, but what if it was in you? Would you stop searching? We look without, because we often feel empty within. We want to be significant and make a difference in the world; so we go in search of the elusive "it," a thing that will make us feel completely whole, lacking the understanding that we came to this planet whole, lacking nothing.

THE ELUSIVE "IT"

The elusive "it" can be described by some as fame and fortune, and for others it is helping and giving so they are seen as a good person. Yet, for others it is drugs, alcohol and sex. No matter what "it" is, we are all in search of it so we will not feel empty and alone. We think that if we could get it, we would be okay, whole and complete. Understand that nothing from the external can fill the vast emptiness of the internal. No matter what we achieve without God, we are still broken.

"It" Has Been Discovered Over 2000 Years Ago

Breaking News, "it" has been found. Yes, reports confirm that "it" was hung on some sticks shaped like a cross on mount Calvary. "It" was hiding in plain sight. "It" was just hanging there in plain view of everyone. The uninformed person booed, hissed and spat on "it." Those who knew what "it" was, bowed and worshipped.

The news has been collaborated by some ancient writing, that "it" was not of this world, "it" came from a far off placed called "The Kingdom of Heaven" where "it" was King of kings and Lord of lords.

Reports say that "it" was a gift-giver, a life-giving presence that when "it" gave up the ghost, the Earth shook, and thunder roared. They took "it" and laid it in a tomb, rolled a stone in front of the tomb to keep "it" from escaping. Guards were placed in front of the tomb to watch "it." "It" must have been something of great value that they went through all that trouble to keep "it" from getting out. There were reports that three days later, a few believers who trusted and followed "it" came to visit. They knew "it" as savior, friend and healer of the sick. When they arrived at the tomb where "it" laid in death, "it" had risen and was gone. They were distraught, shaken and felt they were robbed. They heard a voice and saw a figure who said, "It had risen."

New information is coming in, "it" was not an "it" but a man and God.

The Promise Fulfilled

Jesus was the promise fulfilled. There is no more need to search for "it." Who you are searching for to give your life significance is Jesus, the artist, potter, creative word, the One who set the stars in the heavens. By His light we walk. His light shines with the intensity of the sun and sparkles like a diamond; His light is perfect and created in perfection (Love).

Jesus has designed our walk with Him in the same manner. Every step has been considered before it was ever made; every problem solved before it came into being; every roadblock removed before we ever traveled the road.

Just like a diamond, we need to be clean thoroughly, cut carefully to shine our brightest. We cannot let the world define or clean us. We need a deep clean, one that is able to reach our soul, and refresh our spirit.

Diamonds From Heaven

We are diamonds from heaven, and like earthly diamonds, we must be fashioned and shaped into precious jewels. We have to be cut, polished and cut repeatedly, until we reach our full brilliance. This process of cutting and polishing is what makes us diamonds so valuable.

A diamond is not pretty in its rawness, and neither are we. Coal is the birthplace of a diamond. With great pressure and much heat, that dark piece of coal becomes hardened into what we call a diamond. Even though it is a diamond by nature, it has not come into its fullness. A diamond must yield itself to the master artisan so that he can shape it into a work of beauty. This process may seem hard or a long journey, but it looks harder than it really is. We must make a conscious effort each moment of the day to stand, knowing we no longer belong to the worldly systems, but we are a New Creation in Christ Jesus.

The directions of our thought must change dramatically. There should no longer be a "me" focus, but a "we" (humanity) focus. The buyer requires that His will be done, along with the fulfillment of your God created purpose which He told through the Scriptures. He died on the cross, so He would be able to relate to the human condition, making Him better at directing our ship.

Humble Yourself

We must become as little children, open minded and trusting the Holy Spirit to work in and through us. We need to humble ourselves, so we can learn from more mature followers of Christ, though age is not always an indicator of maturity. We can judge maturity by their walk and fruit. I am amazed at how many age-old followers of Jesus are on milk and still crawling, yet they refuse to accept that they have not grown in years.

This journey is perfected in love, filled with grace and mercy, which renews daily. We can stand before God in faith, trusting our Lord without wavering, knowing we are more than conquerors (See Romans 8:37).

A sign of our maturity comes when we are comfortable with surrendering the direction of our present situation (life) to the Lord and Him alone. It is not ours to fight alone; we are in direct relationship with the King of heaven and the entire universe. We are not alone, ever.

We no longer reach for our old ways of warfare, but we are holding on to Christ as we come to realize that God is real, not because a preacher told us, but because we have experienced His love personally. We have experienced that life-giving power that closed the mouth of fear, doubt and want. We are royalty, covered in the blood of Jesus, and united with Him forever.

BATTLEFIELDS OF LIFE

We have to know that we are victorious by faith in Christ Jesus, and no enemy can overtake us. Always trusting that God will deliver our enemy to us, we hear Jesus say, *"Sit and eat, this battle has already been fought and won, and the enemies you see today, you will see no more forever."*

We know that through Jesus, we are more than a conqueror, and greater is He who is in us, than any enemy we face in this world.

We must walk by faith on this journey. This journey allows us to walk on water, above sin, shame, fear and even death. Despite our circumstances, we must trust in Jesus the Christ, and not our present situation, or our current aches and pains. He is always near. We just need to call His name, Jesus.

We must trust and hold to the fact that every step we take with Jesus is on solid ground, even when the ground beneath our feet starts to move. We need to trust the quality of our seed of faith, not the environment, or what we see and hear. We cannot rely on our five senses, and even our own understanding of the matter is a weak defense.

On this journey, our refuge, strong fortress, and hedge of protection is, and will always be, our faith and trust in Jesus, who is the Author and Finisher, the Alpha and Omega, the One who planned for every situation, the One who gave us a way of escape, the One who gave His life so that we might live in freedom.

If we can obey the Master, move when He says move, hold when He says hold, we will slay dragons, walk on water and eat the good of the land.

The journey is not always easy. Our flesh is constantly at war against following the leading of the Holy Spirit. The flesh wants to be satisfied and have its way. We can, and we must, overcome the desire to let our feelings direct us. Raw emotions and flesh can never please God.

Chapter 1 Outro

Do not give away your seed for a moment of pleasure. Do not give away your legacy for a taste of sweet revenge, which in the end is death to you and your future seed. Do not fall into the trap that you cannot be like God. You are made in the image and likeness of God. The enemy Satan is always working to confuse your identity. You are like God, that is how you were created. Surrender your will to the Father and fall into the arms of Jesus. He loves you and has a great future planned for you. You did not and could not die for yourself, but Jesus did. He gave you His reward in exchange for your reward.

Chapter 1 Take Away

1. **Understanding is defined as** *information that a person can stand under.* When you truly understand something, it covers you. If you lack understanding, you are exposed. What you don't know can and will hurt you.

2. **Time is your most valuable asset, so treat it as such.** Time does not differ for anyone. We have the same number of hours per day, the same number of minutes and seconds. Where we spend it determines what we value. Learn to make the time you have work for you.

Don't squander the moments; once they are gone, they are gone forever.

3. **The directions of our thought must change dramatically** from a "me" focus, to a "we" (humanity) focus. The journey is about growing into the person God called you to be. Your thoughts will always come before your actions. Change your thoughts and you will change your life. You are not here for you alone; you are here for me and I am here for you. We were created to be in a community.

4. **This process may seem hard and difficult. The journey looks harder than it really is.** The problem for all is surrendering self and will to the process of change. The journey is designed to teach, grow, refine and produce God-like fruit. Embrace the changes with an attitude of gratitude and know in the end that it was all for your good.

CHAPTER 2

Relationship: The One Who Should Matter The Most

Relationship: *connecting or binding participants in a relationship, where both parties benefit from the union, but not always equally.*

THE FIRST RELATIONSHIP

*H*ow did we get here? We are all the product of a relationship; good, bad, or a one-night event. Our natural journey into the Earth realm was by relationship (sexual relationship). Everything we know, we learned from one of our relationships. The first relationship we encounter is usually with our mother, father or caregiver. We learn how to connect to others based on how our first relationship connects with us. We develop our inside voice by our outside relationships. Our relationships become the rudder that steers our life from afar.

The relationships we have in our formative years creates our perspective, identity and worldview. Inadequate relationships in the beginning will yield in us a sense of inadequacy. We feel that something must be wrong with us since our first relationship was not stable, trustworthy, loving or abusive. Our first relationships often create the template for our future relationships. We develop our present relationships based on our first relationships. Our first relationship with the opposite sex, for example, a father, becomes the prototype for relationships; good, bad or indifferent. This could be the reason there are so many failed relationships in society. Because the first relationship failed, the individual never developed a solid identity of who they are.

A Better Plan For Us

God has a better plan for us. God is always just, always present, He never sleeps. He knows what we think, and He knows the beginning from the end. God's very nature and essence is love, and He cares for us deeply.

Love is what drives relationships. We say we fall in and out of it, as if it was a thing that we could fall in and out of like a bed, chair or car. However, love is not such a thing; love is action. We do for others because we love them. We protect them because we love them.

If we as humans can give to others because we love them, then how much more can God give to us? He is not sharing love like we do; He is love, and nothing about Him is anything other than love. This loving God is seeking a relationship with us, so why would we refuse to have such a relationship with a God who is pure love. He is not showing love, but He is love. God loves us, so how else can one express love but to give? We give to those we love, so why would Love not give to us? God loves us so much that He gave His only begotten son (See John 3:16).

Consider for a moment the one thing you treasure. Take that one thing you treasure and give it to a drunk, murdering, trouble-making person, just to show love to them. Most of us would not dare give away something so valuable to someone so undeserving. We would probably be reluctant to show love in that way, yet God gave knowing that we are not worthy.

RELATIONSHIP WITH GOD

God is looking for a relationship with us, but are we looking for one with Him? If we are willing to seek a real relationship with God and to know His ways, God promised to give us all things.

A relationship with God should not be built on what we can get, but on giving. God is love. He will give because that is His nature. We would not exist if God was not love. He gave us His Son before we were born, so we could have the opportunity of a better life.

Do not think that God requires your love, because He does not. He wants your love. Think of it this way; if you are a typical person in a relationship, not for love, but because it was required for you to get what you needed to survive, that is not a true relationship of love. Relationships like those, or arrangements, often end due to one or both parties feeling obligated without the freedom of choice.

Now think of being in a relationship because you want to be, and the other person want it as well. Both of you will want to give to the relationship, not out of necessity, but out of love.

No matter how you came to be, it started with two ships having some form of a relationship. That is the process to get you from there to here. We are not concerned with your birthing ship or your donating ship; we are concerned about you. Parentage is a topic for another book, or another chapter. In retrospect, we came to earth by way of relationship; some by game, some with violence, some with pain but kept silent, and some with love. Most of us just happened or so it would seem. Single parent households seem to be the norm, at least on my side of the world.

Nevertheless, we are here now, and we need to make our way from our birth to His glory. How we got here was just the beginning of our story.

God Dropped Jesus

Jesus came the same way. God dropped Jesus into a virgin vessel, so He could be born of a woman. He experienced every temptation and overcame them, so He could bring us back into a right relationship with the Father. He wanted to be with us so much that He came as one of us, to teach us what it would take to be in a relationship with the Father. Since none of us was without sin, God sent us His only begotten Son, Jesus. What an honor it is to be in relationship with the living God. Jesus came to show us the way, and all we need to do is follow and obey.

Before we go too far from purpose and let life cause us to stray, I want to tell you that your journey begins with a relationship with God, the Father, through the Son, Jesus the Christ. We did not come here alone, and we cannot make it here alone.

> *Whoever transgresses and does not abide in the doctrine of Christ does not have God. He who abides in the doctrine of Christ has both the Father and the Son. (2 John 1:9).*

Watchman Nee writes, *"Over-sensitivity is another trait at which generally marks the soulish. Very difficult are they to live with because they interpret every move around them as aimed at them. When neglected they become angry. When they suspect changing attitudes towards them, they are hurt. They easily become intimate with people, for they literally thrive on such affection. They exhibit the sentiment of inseparability. A slight change in such a relationship will give their soul unutterable pains. And thus, these people are deceived into thinking they are suffering for the Lord."*

DEFINE RELATIONSHIPS

Here is how Webster's dictionary define relationships:

> n. An interpersonal relationship is a strong, deep, or close association or acquaintance between two or more people that may range in duration from brief to enduring. This association mostly based on inference, love, solidarity, regular business interactions, or some other type of social commitment.

Pyschologytoday.com has an area called, **"All About Relationships."** This is what they have to say about relationships:

> "Love is one of the most profound emotions known to human beings. There are many kinds of love, but most people seek its expression in a romantic relationship with a compatible partner. Those relationships are not destiny, but they appear to establish patterns of relating to others."

Let us not forget our definition of Relationship: *connecting or binding participants in a relationship.* God is looking for a deep eternal relationship with us. *What are you looking for from God?*

As we look at the definitions, we can see that for a relationship to begin there needs to be some type of association, either from friendship, or a common circumstance like a team, platoon, classmates or business. We ought to know that a relationship can and will develop from associating with anyone over time. To have a meaningful, solid and lasting relationship, a few things should be present: common aim, common values and common understanding of self and others.

WHO ARE THEY?

It is easy to see a person when life is the wind beneath their wings, and they are soaring. Most people are happy and full of joy in those times. But who are they when the wind that was lifting them high becomes the wind that is pushing them low? We want to seek first to understand them, if we expect them to understand us.

SEE HIM AS HE IS

God knows that for you to understand Him, you must first see Him as He is. Our hearts must change to see that God is love. God knows us because He made us. God is not looking to fix you, because you are not broken. What is broken is your identity, your vision, your relationship to your source; that is broken, but you are not. There is nothing wrong with your soul, but your life is broken due to your misalignment, false identity and blurred vision. God does not think you are broken, or worthless. He wants to fix your vision, so you will see yourself and others the way He does; valuable and worthy of love.

GOAL OF THE RELATIONSHIP

The goal of any good relationship is to deposit more than you withdraw. Jesus did just that by giving us His life, so that we may have a better life and a lasting, deep, eternal relationship with Father God, through Him. What more could we give? He gave His life that we might live. All He asks in return is that we obey, walk in faith and love Him with all our mind and soul. How hard is it to give what was freely given to you?

If we want to have a true, eternal relationship with the Father, we must be willing to give something of significant value. Do we need to sacrifice our first-born to show God that we love Him? Do we need to give up all our earthly possessions? Maybe God the Father is asking for our happiness, fashion, style and free will. What is that high-sought value that we need to give to please God? That value is our time, faith, and love. In order to get all that God has for us, we must give our time, faith and love.

BEAUTY FOR ASHES

Let us hear the offer again; God is asking for our time, faith and love in exchange for the keys to His Kingdom. God is saying to us, "I will give you beauty for ashes." (See Isaiah 61:3). Let us use our imagination here for a moment, God is telling us, in my own words, *"Give me your burnt up, worthless house and I will give you a brand-new custom one in its place."* God is requesting your beat-up car and He is going to give you a brand new custom made one designed perfectly for you. That is what love looks like when God is the giver.

Deuteronomy 4:29 tells us what we need to do to seek a relationship with the Father:

> *But from there you will seek the Lord your God, and you will find Him if you seek Him with all your heart and with all your soul.*

Jesus tells us in *Matthew 22:37* how we are to love the Lord:

> *Jesus said to him, "You shall love the Lord your God with all your heart, with all your soul, and with all your mind."*

Luke takes it a step further and tells us how to love the Lord God, and how we are to love one another, and not be envious, jealous, or lustful towards one another. We are to love one another as we love ourselves.

THE PERSON ON THE STREET

We tend to exhibit love to others in the manner in which we have experienced love by man and not as God has loved us. Those demonstrations of love that we witnessed, experienced, or heard through the years are less than what we know of God.

The assumption here is that even a person on the street deserves to be shown love. As humans, we have a joint relationship with them through Christ Jesus, because we are the hands and feet of the living God. We are not incapable of displaying true AGAPE love to someone we just met. We can love someone with whom we do not have a relationship. The only way we can love the world is through Christ, for without Christ, it is impossible to love the people of the world properly, and unconditionally.

Here is what Luke wrote about the matter of love:

> *And behold, a certain lawyer stood up and tested Him, saying, "Teacher, what shall I do to inherit eternal life?" He said to him, "What is written in the law? What is your reading of it?" So he answered and said, "'You shall love the Lord your God with all your heart, with all your soul, with all your strength, and with all your mind,' and 'your neighbor as yourself.'" And He said to him, "You have answered rightly; do this and you will live." (Luke 10:25-28)*

Jesus is calling us to an eternal relationship, one that is not marred by events or broken by missteps and varied misunderstandings, but shaped and strengthened over time as we walk with Him through the journey of our life. We have to be willing to give Jesus our all, if we expect all from Him. Our goal and desire should be one of giving, sharing and helping the less fortunate.

Unfortunately, many of us did not have someone to care for us properly, so we grew up slanted, skewed, warped, or off-balanced in what we thought about love, care and relationships.

Sometimes the person who said they loved us ended up taking more than they gave, and we grew up feeling that we are owed something.

Life cycles in and out of seasons, so we will find ourselves in a season where we are on the receiving or giving end more than we may be comfortable with. Regardless of what season we are in, our hearts and minds should always be focused on Christ, and our desire should be to give generously and joyfully. Giving should be our pleasure, not a chore.

Always Desire To Give

Here is an illustration of why we should always desire to give and give generously. As children, we were not able to care for ourselves in any fashion. We depended on someone else for our basic care for the first few years of our life. We could not do anything for ourselves.

As time went on, we grew up and began to learn some things, for example, how to sit up, and how to comfort ourselves. We eventually learned how to feed ourselves, crawl, stand up, walk and talk. Then the moment came when we felt like we had arrived at the elusive place known as independence. We learned how to dress ourselves and tie our shoes.

Leave Me Alone

We would sometimes say, *"Leave me alone. I know how to do it."* We knew we were ready to be independent because time reveals all our strengths and weakness. When we met on a problem we did not have an answer for, we hated the feeling of needing someone else. We wanted to be independent and would sometimes lie by saying, *"I got it"* when we were not even close to having it.

These are stages of growth. Before we could do anything, we had to depend on someone else to do them for us. Once we had grown up we were expected to make good choices based on the teaching we have been giving. God has set options before us as well, choices. We fall into situations because we choose them, God set's in front of us all life and death, blessings and curses. We are expected to choose life.

> *See, I have set before you today life and good, death and evil, in that I command you today to love the Lord your God, to walk in His ways, and to keep His commandments, His statutes, and His judgments, that you may live and multiply; and the Lord your God will bless you in the land which you go to possess. I call heaven and earth as witnesses today against you, that I have set before you life and death, blessing and cursing; therefore choose life, that both you and your descendants may live; that you may love the Lord your God, that you may obey His voice, and that you may cling to Him, for*

He is your life and the length of your days; and that you may dwell in the land which the Lord swore to your fathers, to Abraham, Isaac, and Jacob, to give them.. (Deuteronomy 30:15-16, 19-20)

Now, It Is Our Turn To Give

A real relationship will not be shallow and engrossed by fulfilling one's personal needs and desires. A real relationship will challenge you to grow beyond your current stage of selfishness.

A real relationship should challenge us to elevate our self-centered mind beyond just our own physiological, social and material needs. The right ordained relationship can take us to new heights of perspective and move us in ways that we did not know was possible by shaping us into a person of greatness. All our relationships are extremely critical in how well we will navigate, grow and face the challenges of life's journey.

Relationships are not equitable in balance. It is not always a 50/50 task or effort.

We do not have the right to become a taker because we have more to give. Here is my perspective; we have more to give because we give. We have planted seeds, so when the time comes, we will reap a harvest. We should not enter any relationship with "me" on the brain. We have to continue to plant good seeds, if we want to reap a good harvest. As long as the earth remains, seedtime and harvest will not cease. If we want a harvest, we will have to plant. One of the ways we plant seeds is through our relationships.

The question remains, why be in a relationship if it is not going to be all about me? The answer; it is not about you. Relationships should be about mutual benefit, respect, understanding, vulnerability and honesty. It is not about you taking from the relationship, but it is about you giving to the relationship.

I have been speaking of relationships as if it is fair and equitable, but it is not. We text more than we study "The Text." Our eyes are not fixed on Jesus. Our eyes are fixed on iPhones and iPads - emphasis on "I."

Mark Batterson wrote:

>*We want character without suffering.*
>
>*We want success without failure.*
>
>*We want gain without pain.*
>
>*We want a testimony without the test.*
>
>*We want it all without going all out for it.*

If we want to be in any relationship, we must spend time understanding the other person, so we are understood by the person we are in a relationship with. God created us, so the time is not for Him to understand us. God will never ask a question He does not already know the answer to. We can make excuses as to why we do not have time to cultivate an honest relationship with others, but why would we not cultivate a relationship with the One who created us? He knows what He has planned for us; we do not. Most of us are stumbling around life as if we are in the dark. God says:

> *For I know the thoughts that I think toward you, says the Lord, thoughts of peace and not of evil, to give you a future and a hope. (Jeremiah 29:11)*

CLOSE TO THE FATHER

Jesus was so close to the Father that He and the Father was One. He was in a right relationship with Him. Jesus said only what He heard the Father say and did only what He saw the Father do. We should only say what we hear the Father saying and only do what we see the Father doing.

> *Then Jesus answered and said to them, "Most assuredly, I say to you, the Son can do nothing of Himself, but what He sees the Father do; for whatever He does, the Son also does in like manner." (John 5:19)*

I think we sometimes forget the part about the need to connect to the vine, who is Jesus. He gave because the Father gave. He healed because the Father is a healer. Then He tells us that we will do greater things than what He did. We are connected one to another; branches of the same vine.

We came to be because our parents had a relationship, whether it was of love or purely sexual. We exist because there was a relational interaction. We are, because God is, and without God, we do not and could not exist. Some of us know people who are looking for fire insurance. For those of us who grew up in and around the church, we know what that means. We get in a relationship with the church, just in case there is something beyond this life. We operate in the church out of duty, just so we can keep up our premiums on the fire insurance. God does not want you to come to Him out of fear, but love. Relations with God is not about fire insurance, it's about life. This is about living this life to the best of our ability so we can have the promise; a life of abundance and purpose.

If you are reading this, and you do not know Jesus or you have never had a real encounter with the true and living God, I want to take this time to lead you in prayer to introduce you to Him. Pray this prayer:

> *Heavenly Father, please forgive me. I know I am a sinner and have fallen short of Your glory. I asked that You come into my life right now that I may grow to know Your Son, Jesus, who died and rose again for me. Jesus, I accept You as my Lord, and Savior, and I seek a personal and true relationship with You. I thank You for it. I receive the gift of salvation and I submit my will to Your Holy Spirit to lead and guide me into truth from this day forward, in Jesus name I pray, Amen.*

If that was the first time you have prayed this prayer, I would now suggest that you seek out a Bible teaching community that is centered on a right relationship with God, and not religion.

Grab a Bible and begin to read it. While you are reading it, imagine the Father right there with you, guiding you into a right relationship with Him.

The first Ship is Relationship. We must master it in order to enjoy this journey called life.

CHAPTER 2 OUTRO

The most important relationship we should seek to have is one with the Father, who made us and ordained us to be. We have all encountered bad relationships at one time or another. God is not fickle like that. He loves us unconditionally. There is nothing we can do to earn His love. We just have to accept the gift and come into a relationship with Him. Knowing God as Lord of our life is the relationship that should matter most in our lives.

Once we have a right relationship with Him, the rest of our relationships should just reflect that right relationship.

CHAPTER 2 TAKE AWAY

1. **We all came to Earth through** some form of a relationship. No one exist without it.

2. **Relationships are not always equitable**; they are rarely 50/50. They should be 100/100.

3. **You came to this planet to fulfill a purpose.** It is not about you. Relationships is a constant reminder that we are to be givers and not just takers.

4. **Once you have a right relationship with the Father**, you can begin to improve your other relationships.

5. **You are made in the image of the Father.** We are like God. Since we are like God, we should display Him in all our relationships. This is the most important aspect of a right relationship, i.e., God's love for us is shared with everyone we encounter.

6. **Are you in a right relationship with the Father?** If not, get into one sooner than later; your eternal life depends on it. Do not come to the Father out of fear but come out love and let Him show you who He created you to be. God is love, so we must show that love to the world.

CHAPTER 3

What Is True Fellowship?

For the first century Christians in the book of Acts, Fellowship included hearing a message, reading the Scriptures aloud, eating a meal together and discussing what they heard and read.

Today, some smaller churches still share in a meal after service. To have truth in Fellowship, we have to share a meal. Prior to the blooming of mega churches, most churches had a meal after the message on Sunday.

> *And they continued steadfastly in the apostles' doctrine and fellowship, in the breaking of bread, and in prayers. (Acts 2:42)*

To have real fellowship, we must have three things; someone to fellowship with, the word of God, and food. The reason these elements are so important is that it allows us to lower our guards and feast with the Lord in truth.

On the matter of fellowship, J.L. Parker wrote:

> *We should not think of our fellowship with other Christians as a spiritual luxury, or an optional addition to the exercises of private devotion. We should recognize rather that such fellowship is a spiritual necessity, for God has made us in such a way that our fellowship with Himself is fed by our fellowship with fellow Christians and, moreover, requires to be so fed constantly for its own deepening and enrichment.*

EAT WHILE YOU NEGOTIATE

Here is an excerpt from a Harvard Business Review titled, "Should You Eat While You Negotiate" by Lakshmi Balachandra:

> *Across cultures, dining together is a common part of the process of reaching negotiated agreements. In Russia and Japan, important business dealings are conducted almost exclusively while dining and drinking and, in the U.S., many negotiations begin with, "Let's do lunch." NEVERTHELESS, business deals have shown to improve when people discuss important matters over a MEAL.*
>
> *To explore this question, I conducted two experiments. The first compared negotiations that took place over a meal in a restaurant, over negotiations in conference rooms without food. In the second negotiations conducted with or without a meal, 132 MBA students*

negotiated a complex joint venture agreement between two companies. In the simulation, a provisional deal is in place, but a variety of terms must still be considered and agreed upon to maximize profits for their companies. The negotiators must determine how to handle each term of the deal. As typical in most negotiations, to maximize their profits, the negotiators must share information and work together with the other side to learn where the most value would be created.

The PARTIES WHO FELLOWSHIPED together over a meal WERE ABLE TO DISCERN THE OTHER SIDES Wants and needs AND THEN WORK COLLECTIVELY, they were able TO DISCOVER a more favorable outcome. They were able to increase PROFIT and MAXIMIZE the overall OUTCOMES FOR THE JOINT VENTURE. Through fellowship they were able to see the other sides point of view. RATHER THAN MERELY CONSIDERING just what mattered to them i.e. THE PROFITS OF THEIR OWN COMPANY CREATED THE GREATEST POSSIBLE PROFITS overall. In the simulation, this would only be accomplished when the negotiators make trade-offs and then compensate each other from the net gains to the joint venture.

The maximum value that can be created jointly for both companies is $75 million. Deals can be struck at lower combined values, down to as low as $38 million. To explore how eating together affected the outcome of *negotiations, I considered the total value created by both companies.*

The students who ate together while negotiating — either at a restaurant or over food brought in — created a more significant profit compared to those who negotiated without dining. (Individuals who negotiated in restaurants created 12% greater profits than those who negotiated over food in a conference room whom created 11% greater profits.) This suggests that eating while deciding important matters offers profitable, measurable benefits through mutually productive discussions.

In CONCLUSION of the experiment, research has shown that the consumption of glucose enhances complex brain activities, bolstering self-control and regulating prejudice and aggressive behaviors. Other research has shown that unconscious mimicking behaviors of others leads to increased pro-social behaviors; when individuals eat TOGETHER, they enact the same movements. This unconscious mimicking of each other may induce positive feelings towards both the other party and the matter under discussion.[1]

---

[1] https://hbr.org/2013/01/should-you-eat-while-you-negot

A MEAL TOGETHER; FELLOWSHIP

What can we learn from having a meal together? To be in true fellowship, we must have a meal together; first the spiritual, then the natural. Many Scriptures speak of Jesus and His disciples having meals together. *Why is this act of eating together so important in building a relationship?* Social science research explores why sitting down to eat together makes people feel closer.

Eating food is about bringing something into the body and lowering our defenses. Eating the same food with another person brings you and that person together in a common act. The meal provides a level of trust as both agree to eat at the same time. Scientific research points to the fact that people feel closer to one another when they are eating the same food at the same time. Because of the meal, trust and cooperation can emerge, which promotes unity and that can bring us closer together.

If you are going through life and you decide to jump on the fellowship boat with another, make sure you are eating the same spiritual food.

> *Can two walk together, unless they are agreed? (Amos 3:3)*

We will look at one Greek word as it relates to Fellowship. But before we study the Greek, what does the English dictionary have to say about fellowship? Let us see how the Merriam-Webster dictionary defines **fellowship:**

> *Companionship, company looking for the fellowship of friendly people.*
>
> *2a: community of interest, activity, feeling, or experience their fellowship in crime — the state of being a fellow or associate.*
>
> *3: a company of equals or friends: association with a youth fellowship.*
>
> *4: the quality or state of being comradely meaningful communication for building trust and fellowship.*
>
> *5: obsolete: membership, partnership*

In the Strong's Concordance, we find the Greek word, *"Koninwnia: koinónia:"* for fellowship:

> *The original word is: κοινωνία, ας, ἡ and the part of speech is Noun, Feminine.*
>
> *Transliteration: koinónia*
>
> *Phonetic Spelling: (koy-nohn-ee'-ah)*
>
> *Short Definition: participation, communion, fellowship*
>
> *Definition: (lit: partnership) (a) contributory help, participation, (b) sharing in, communion, (c) spiritual fellowship, a fellowship in the spirit.*

If we were to dissect the English dictionary's meaning of Fellowship, we would see three common parts. Firstly, fellowship means being part of a group, or a body of people. It is opposed to isolation, solitude, and loneliness as our present-day independent kind of individualism would suggest. Secondly, fellowship means having or sharing parts of our lives with people, such as things in common: beliefs, activities, labor, and responsibilities -- our experiences and concerns. Thirdly, fellowship can also mean a partnership that involves working together and caring for one another as a company of people, for example, a company of soldiers or members of a family.

In the early church, what was Luke saying when he said:

> *And they continued steadfastly in the apostles' doctrine and fellowship, in the breaking of bread, and in prayers. (Acts 2:42).*

What is the point and the message here? In order for us to gain a deeper understanding of what Luke was talking about, we must study the Greek word mentioned above: **Koniwn,** *the root word is* **koinos**: meaning *common, mutual, public.*

The main idea conveyed by the word "koinos" is having something in common, sharing ideas, or things and giving to others our cooperation in a partnership of sorts. Therefore, the question remains, in whom are we sharing fellowship? Does it matter what we share and with whom we share?

> *If we say that we have fellowship with Him, and walk in darkness, we lie and do not practice the truth. But if we*

walk in the light as He is in the light, we have fellowship with one another, and the blood of Jesus Christ His Son cleanses us from all sin. (I John 1:6-7).

It seems that common or commonality fits in this verse, but does that tell us what fellowship is supposed to be in our lives today? I would like to suggest that it does and here is how; we are supposed to be common with our brothers and sisters in Christ, but what does that mean using the Greek word *koinos*?

Original Word: κοινός, ή, όν

Part of Speech: Adjective

Transliteration: koinos

Phonetic Spelling: (koy-nos')

FELLOWSHIP: SHORT DEFINITION: COMMON, SHARED, AND UNCLEAN

When we are in true fellowship with someone, we are going to share something together and we are going to come unclean, not in the sense of being dirty, but rather in the sense of being bare, real, and raw; we are going to show our true identity. We are going to show our vulnerabilities to one another, and we are going to share our weaknesses, fears, doubts, and shame with one another. That is true fellowship and I believe most heart to heart conversations or business deals and major opportunities usually take place over a meal, while sharing in each other's lives. Think of how much better life would be if there were no "**Facebook living**."

Facebook living is where you only show your best, and perfect the art of only telling what sounds good, showing only the best parts of life that make you look good to others and never the real. In reality, you need something which is honest and real.

We always want to look our best in the eyes of others, never wanting to be raw, real and transparent. We refuse to let others in on our troubles so they can help us carry our load, for example, our pain, doubts, fears, insecurities, and flawed families.

We as believers are supposed to find trustworthy brothers and sisters to whom we can confess our shortcomings and issues that are so common to so many living on this side of salvation.

Fellowship is about eating, drinking, thinking, and sharing all that life has to offer with a group of like-hearted people in the spirit of commonality, while learning, growing in the grace, knowledge, and the truth of Jesus the Christ.

We are not alone, even though we are born alone and die alone, as it would seem, but God never meant for us to live and manage life alone.

> *Finally, all of you be of one mind, having compassion for one another; love as brothers, be tenderhearted, be courteous; not returning evil for evil or reviling for reviling, but on the contrary blessing, knowing that you*

were called to this, that you may inherit a blessing. (1 Peter 3:8-9)

That which we have seen and heard we declare to you, that you also may have fellowship with us; and truly our fellowship is with the Father and with His Son Jesus Christ. (1 John 1:3)

LIFE

I am a painting, that hasn't been painted,

A moving fixture, a still picture in constant motion.

I am laughing cries and cheerful sighs.

Large rivers with tiny oceans;

I am a shallow lake with a mile-deep stream,

Answers with no questions

Solutions with no problems

Rounded squares and cornered circles, responsibilities with no cares

Death visits me daily, but never will I die.

I am dark as light and bright as night, a slave that is free.

A strong wind that never blows

Dreams are my reality.

Ups that go down and downs that go up, left that goes right

I am a narrow path that is wide, a steep hill that is a flat plain.

Happiness that is sad, richness that is poor

All the things you understood and everything you could not explain.

I am all that you thought and nothing you could imagine.

I am Life.

CALL ON HIM IN THE STORM

Storms will come, and the clouds will attempt to hide the Son, Jesus, from our view. But I know one ship that comes with a joy, peace, hope, and a love so divine, that it will feed thousands, open the ears of the deaf and the eyes of the blind. This ship is called Jesus the Christ, and He will never steer us wrong, no matter how troubled the waves. He died before we came into existence, and He calmed the roughest of seas so that we could be free.

When looking for fellowship, look first to Jesus the Christ. Fellowship with the Lord of lords and King of kings is required on this journey. Who else would have hung on a cross so that we might choose to fellowship with the Father? Who else has proven repeatedly that He is our closest of friends? Even when we deserved death, and up to our neck in sin, He gave His life that we might have life more abundantly. No one could do all that, but Jesus the Christ.

The Ship of Fellowship is required to navigate the waters of change, fear, doubts, and uncertainty. The only One who knows the beginning from the end is the One who sets the stars in place and spoke Light into existence; the Father God. The only way to the Father is through the Son, Jesus Christ. We grow closer to the Father by fellowshipping with Jesus and other believers. Through consistent fellowship, we shed our false self and show our true selves that they may come to know us, and we know them as Christ knows us all, in spirit and in truth; nothing hidden.

> *If we say that we have fellowship with Him, and walk in darkness, we lie and do not practice the truth. But if we walk in the light as He is in the light, we have fellowship with one another, and the blood of Jesus Christ His Son cleanses us from all sin. (I John 1:6-7).*

Let us get in right fellowship with the Father through the Son, that we may break bread with Him daily and in doing that, we become partakers of the cross.

PRAYER TO ACCEPT CHRIST

Father in heaven, give us this day our daily provision. Forgive us as we forgive them that have counted us down and out. Forgive us for our fears and doubts and lead us to the well of determination. Let us drink from the rivers of life that changes us from the inside out.

Open our eyes so we can see the world through Your eyes of creation and not our lens of fear and doubt. Lead us not into temptation, but deliver us from the spirit of quitting, falling back or passivity in our current situation. Give us courage to stand up for ourselves and the less fortunate.

Let the light that You have placed in us illuminate the darkness in our lives. Change our mind from one of impossibilities to one of possibilities. Let us not focus on what we do not have but learn to be thankful for what we do have.

Give us the strength to be bold and the courage to be who You created us to be and not copies of who we thought we were. Let Your creative spirit flow through us so we can create a better world for ourselves through our spoken word. For we are created in Your image and in You there is no lack; in You there is no fear. Show us now this day how to be more like You and less like the fallen man.

We are whole because You are whole; we are holy because You are holy. We give You all the honor and praise for You are the Author and Finisher of our faith. Forever and ever. Amen.

Chapter 3 Outro

Fellowship is necessary for everyone. God did not design us to do life alone. He made us with a desire to spend time with people. This need to fellowship may be the reason families who eat dinner together have been shown to have a deeper relationship.

Fellowship is not just about spending time together, it's about eating and being honest while spending time. We know that fellowship was very important to the early church. It was a command that Jesus left them at the last supper.

What the modern church calls communion is not just about remembering what Christ did on Calvary, it is also about us coming together in common unity to remind ourselves that we are to be like Jesus and we too should pour ourselves out for our fellow human. We are to fellowship with one another often and when we do, let it be in honesty and truth.

Chapter 2 Take Away

1. **Fellowship does not take place without the breaking of bread** and eating a meal together.

2. **Fellowship should be open and honest** for it to be true fellowship. Both parties must be raw if they are going to share in fellowship.

3. **The most important fellowship** we should all consider is fellowshipping with Jesus the Christ.

Chapter 4

The Power of Real Friendship

Nothing in life is ever easy but working for it is always a journey worth taking. My challenge to you or, should I say, I dare you to be the friend that you desire to have today.

The Christ, known as Jesus, sticks closer than any brother. He is a friend indeed. He gave up His throne, so we can feed on His flesh and drink His blood. He did not ask if we deserved life, He simply gave His so we would know the true definition of a friend.

As we go along our journey, let us consider with whom we will keep company. In this life, we may never meet a man who would willingly give his life to save ours. Yet, Jesus went to the cross for that very person, for us. I know the only reason I have breath is because Christ gave up His for me. I have seen firsthand what a true friend He is.

When I was born, my lungs would not fill with air. Prayers went up and life came down, so I know that Jesus wears the crown. Jesus took the hit and allowed me to remain. Knowing, acknowledging, and trusting the way He moves me in and out of life's trials and tribulations, I am a living witness that friendship with Christ is truly a rewarding one. Therefore, I give what I have to them that are less fortunate, because my friend, Jesus, gave what He had to me, His Life.

> *The righteous should choose his friends carefully, for the way of the wicked leads them astray. (Proverbs 12:26)*

TO BE A FRIEND

What does it mean to be a friend? Social media tells us that friends are people you have in your network, but those are not friends. Some of the people in your social media group may be good people, but most of them are not your true friend. They are not the ones who will lift you up when you fall or keep you warm when you are cold. Friend is a unique word and the dictionary defines friend in the following manner: *one attached to another by affection or esteem; one who is not hostile.* That is really how Webster's dictionary defines a friend. One of my favorite rap groups, Whodini, had a song called 'Friends' and some of the lyrics are as follows:

> *Friends, how many of us have them?*
>
> *Friends, ones we can depend on*
>
> *Friends, how many of us have them?*

Friends, before we go any further

Let's be friends.

"Friends" is a word we use daily and most of the time we use it in the wrong way. The dictionary does not know the meaning of friends and if you asked me, I could not be much help because a friend is someone you discover for yourself.

Being a friend is more than sending a friend request on social media sites like Facebook and LinkedIn. Receiving likes or reposts on your daily submissions does not constitute a friend. A real friend cares too much and too deeply to see you self-destruct without, at least, saying something. A true friend will not go along with wrongdoing without saying anything.

> *A man who has friends must himself be friendly, but there is a friend who sticks closer than a brother. (Proverbs 18:24).*

A friend who sticks closer than a brother means that when everyone has left you and your back is against the wall, a friend will be there by your side to guide you, encourage you, and assist you in every way possible.

Can we really be friends with Jesus? Jesus is just that type of friend. The first step is for us to deposit the seed of friendship to harvest the fruit of friendship. Not every seed will return bountiful in an harvest, but you may receive more than expected based on your investment.

The one thing we must always consider when planting is the ground in which we cast our seed. All ground is not fertile ground for every type of seed. Therefore, we must cultivate the ground to receive the seed. The nature of the seed determines what it produces. The seed of true friendship can only produce friends. We must be a friend to see if the ground, i.e. the person, is good ground for a true friendship harvest. Today, in our modern world, we take friendship for granted. This is not how the Bible describes a friend. It was Henry Ford who said, *"My best friend is the one who brings out the best in me."*

If we are honest with ourselves, most of our so-called friends do not bring out the best in us. On the contrary, they bring out the worst. We become competitive, depressed, and envious of how they appear to be living. Notice I said, "appear to be living." Most people are Facebook living, it is a façade for what they want the world to think. Why pretend to be a friend in order to gain something? If you are a real friend, it is a free gift.

FRIENDSHIPS ARE OFTEN TESTED

> *Are You not our God, who drove out the inhabitants of this land before Your people Israel, and gave it to the descendants of Abraham Your friend forever? (2 Chronicles 20:7)*

We can infer from the above verse that God wants a relationship with us, so that we may have a friendship with Him. I have heard people say, *"If you have two good friends in this life, you are doing good."* A friend is one of the rarest of all relationships that two people can have outside of a marriage between man and woman.

In order to know anyone or anything requires time spent getting to know and understand. You need to spend time with your friend, Jesus. Talk to Him, read the Bible and other books that are about Him, and pray. He knows you and He wants you to know Him.

A friend is someone to cherish. Jesus is such a friend. He is waiting for us to invest in the friendship by cultivating the relationship that He has prepared. Ann Landers writes, *"Love is friendship that has caught fire. It is quiet understanding, mutual confidence, sharing and forgiving. It is loyalty through good and bad times. It settles for less than perfection and makes allowances for human weaknesses."*

A Praiseworthy Friend

We do not know how to, or we refuse to, submit to one another as Christ submitted Himself to the Father. How can we be a friend to a stranger, if we are not a friend of our brother and Lord, Jesus?

If we are honest with ourselves, we are not praiseworthy friends. How do we become a praiseworthy friend? Think of the friendship between Jesus and His disciples. He was friendly with those men and women. As He spent time with them daily, a friendship developed. The Bible openly states that He has made us friends. He, the Master, has shared His knowledge with us. We are no longer servants but friends (See John 15:15).

What does it mean to love and be a friend? I do not believe you can be a true friend without love, but you can love and not be a friend. Authentic friendships will force us to expose a part of ourselves that few people know exist. A friend will know our character flaws and love us despite those flaws. I am sure we all want others to know us as we are and accept us for being who we are.

We should seek to become our best self and not as the fallen man. The fallen man is not the real us, but an impostor who forces us to put on a facade to hide our brokenness, wounds, and fear of change.

A real friend will know this about us and tell us we are tripping and need to get it together. There is no judgement, no condemnation, just telling the truth to us in love; that is what a real friend would do. They will know our fears, hear our doubts, see our pains and know our truths, and still trust us.

Now, are you such a friend? Do not answer too quickly. Think about it! *Do you have such a friend?* When you think of a friend, what do you consider as non-negotiable requirements? Do you require something of your friend? How do you behave as a friend?

I have friends who will give me a place to stay if I needed it, or give me money, if there is a need. But I do not know any friends who would take care of my family if I passed on. I do not know any friend who would take in my children and raise them as their own. I would like to think that I am such a friend, but the truth is, I do not know what I would do in such a situation.

To The Cross

Jesus called on His friends in the Garden of Gethsemane to watch and pray with Him. I can only imagine how He felt when His friends and partners for the last three years had fallen asleep during His darkest hour. This demonstrates how fickle we are as people.

What are we to do when our friends hurt us, not on purpose, but in the middle of our pain? What do we do when we have given all and they have returned little to nothing? These questions are personal and can only be answered by you.

A friend should be like the stern of a boat. They should help you navigate the rough waters of life. We are capable of being a friend, but we are just selfish by worldly nature and we were taught to be selfish by hurting people and unfair circumstances.

Our current society, with all the technology, advancements in medical treatments, electric cars, and touch-screen phones, have made us a group of people who would rather watch life from a distance, than be involved. We are self-made people, and we do not want to feel like we owe anyone anything. What a lie to tell ourselves so we can feel superior to someone. We do this because we feel inadequate as a person on the inside. There is a void that nothing but the love of the Father, through Christ Jesus, can fill.

What a great lie we fashion for the world; the lie we tell ourselves that, *"We don't need anyone."* Yet, we are lonely and starving for a touch, longing for someone to hold us, longing to be moved by something or someone. We have heard the lies spewed into us since we were babies by the noise of the day, *"You are alone. You don't need them. You can do this by yourself."*

THE MOST IMPORTANT PERSON IN THE ROOM

NEWS FLASH, regardless of who you are, the most important person in the room is the one you are looking to for help; the one you are depending on to provide you an answer, solution, or insight to a situation.

Despite what society has told us, we depend on other people for just about everything. We need people to kill and package the food we eat. Someone is sewing the clothes we wear. Some of us depend on people to bring us to and from our places of employment via public transportation.

When was the last time you hunted for and grow the food you eat? When was the last time you assembled the car you drive or built the house you live in? You see, we depend on others to help us live life better. You will only rise to the level of your five closest friends.

Ali needed Frazier to become a better boxer, just as you need someone to make you better. How far will we rise, if we don't have real friends? We need people at every phase of our life. We need a real friend; someone who will tell us when are wrong, off track and out of order.

GODLY FRIENDSHIPS

The following statements can be a death sentence to a true Godly friendship, if they stand alone. We need to put them in a proper context.

"**You are a star,**" but you will need a supporting cast, so treat people right. God created us in His image, so we do contain greatness. We are all custom made, no two of us are alike. Just like the stars in the sky, we are all different.

"**You can do this by yourself,**" depending on what it is. You need someone to walk alongside you to encourage you when you get weak, and you will get weak. Look for strong people with depth of character.

For us to make it through the day, we need people to help us along the way. You need him, her, the countless others, and people you may never see face to face to help you navigate life. They need you, and I need you as well. We cannot do life alone and say we are followers of Christ.

God created a system of inner-dependence. We need Christ to live, move, and we need each other to cope, survive, enjoy and endure everyday life. No matter how rich we become, without the aid of someone else, it would never have happened. **STOP** thinking you are supposed to be alone. STOP thinking of self as the only one who matters.

You must become friends with yourself. Learn who you are and know yourself well. Seek to make friends with others who are like-minded and moving in a direction that will lead you closer and into a deeper relationship with the Father, God, through Jesus Christ. The goal is to become so involved with the Father that He can call you friend. You have a gift that the world needs, and this gift is not yours alone. You are a steward of the gift so, make a friend and be a friend so you both can be better for the encounter.

The Move

Justin was just a young boy about the age of ten when he moved into a new neighborhood. There was no corner store to hang out in anymore. Justin was accustomed to hanging out at a corner store after school talking to the shopkeepers, Mr. and Mrs. Schwartz. There was no playground two blocks over from his best friend Jennifer and her twin brother Jason. There was no best friend and her twin brother anymore. There was nothing. Everything had changed, and Justin did not like it at all.

Nothing looked the same. Nothing felt familiar. Everything had changed. Justin got out of the car at their new home in Blaine, Minnesota. Justin's father had been transferred there for a four-year assignment by his employer in Miami, Florida. Justin could not help but think of how much he was going to miss the beach, the sunshine, Jennifer, and Jason. They unpacked the car and started moving things into their new home. Justin looked around and became more homesick.

That night, Justin's mom came in from the store and asked him what she could do to make it better? Justin, without even looking up and before she could get the last words out of her mouth, said, "Move back to Miami."

His mother answered, "Sure, as soon as your father's assignment is over."

Justin felt tricked and grumbled, "Mom, that will take forever."

In a stern but playful tone, Justin's mother joked, "I dare you to make one new friend this weekend."

Justin replied, "Mom, you can't dare."

"Justin, I dare you to make the best of our time here and make one new friend this weekend."

Justin was never one to back down from a dare. He said, "Ok, Mom, I will see your dare with making two new friends this week."

The next day, Justin saw two kids playing catch, and he walked over and said, "Hello, my name is Justin."

The two just continued to play catch without even looking his way. Justin was a little irritated to say the least, he said, "Hello, my name is Justin."

Justin was frustrated at the fact that they were ignoring him, so he walked closer to the point where he was standing between the two. Justin said, "Sorry to interrupt, but I just moved here from Miami. We live across the street in the gray castle looking house."

"The previous owners told us that you would be moving in," said one of the kids. The other kid took off his cap and shook his head. He had long black hair. What Justin thought was a he was actually a she. He met Lisa and Lori that day. They were from Brazil and had moved there about twelve years ago when their father's job moved to the states. Lisa and Lori were just beautiful. They loved sports, just like Justin. By that time, he was feeling all right about the move. Justin's mom called him on his cell and told him to come in for dinner. He told his mom, "I am making good on your dare. I just made two new friends, Lisa and Lori, and their family is from Brazil."

Lisa and Lori smiled and said, "Sure, Justin from Miami." They giggled as they walked Justin to the end of their yard. Justin was in heaven. He had never met beautiful girls that were into sports like that. Most of the girls in Miami who were beautiful hated most sports. Justin was glad they moved, because he met two new potential friends.

One of the most overlooked beauties of life is that every day is a new opportunity to do life better. What an awesome thing; to have new grace made available each day. Change often presents a new chance to be better. Look for the opportunity that change offers and make a point to do the impossible.

I dare you to make one new friend this week. Become friends with yourself. Once you make friends with yourself, then seek to know Jesus better each day. Let Him be the friend He desires to be; One who sticks closer than a brother. We are never waiting on the Lord; He is often waiting on us to accept His invitation to a deeper more meaningful relationship with Him, and He desires to call us friend.

Will you let God be a friend to you in every meaning of the word today?

CHAPTER 4 OUTRO

Despite what the noise of the day is yelling, we all need a friend to help us navigate the trials of life. The first friend we should make is with ourselves and the second is with our Lord Jesus Christ.

Don't let selfish ambition keep you from becoming the person God created you to be. Take the time to learn who you are and become your best self. When you discover who you are, don't go through life alone without a friend. Let Jesus be your first friend after yourself.

Chapter 4 Take Away

1. **The goal is to become so involved with the Father** that He can call you friend.

2. **STOP thinking of self** as the only one who matters.

3. **God created a system of inner-dependence.** We need Christ to live, move, and we need each other to cope, survive, enjoy and endure everyday life.

4. **We should seek to become our best self** and not as the fallen man. The fallen man is not the real us, but an impostor who forces us to put on a facade to hide our brokenness, wounds, and fear of change.

5. **Nothing in life is ever easy** but working for it is always a journey worth taking. My challenge to you or, should I say, I dare you to be the friend that you desire to have today.

CHAPTER 5

Discipleship: Learning From the Master

If we are to understand discipleship, we should first understand what it is to be a follower of someone or an idea. Some define discipleship as the process of following the ideas and philosophy of another. I want to define it more like this; *to disciple is to be a student of a pioneer of a particular teaching or of an idea that is not limited to the time and methods in which the concept was first introduced.*

Technology improves the methods we implore to deepen our understanding of the concepts which aid us in being able to explain God's concepts to non-scientific people more effectively. As a disciple of the sciences, we must discipline ourselves in our approach and methods, staying true to the principles set out by the originator of the idea, for example, Isaac Newton. However, we can add to the concept through revelation, leveraging new information that relates to the idea. In doing that, we must stay true to the spirit of the concept, updating it so we can make the content applicable to the time and culture we are in without losing the heart and spirit of the lesson. That is what it means to be a disciple. We must discipline ourselves in following the methods, but it does not mean we are not thinking and seeking to understand more on the subject.

Here is an example: the teachings of Jesus are timeless. The first rule is to follow the ideas and truths of a person or concept so close that we can be ambassadors and not lose the spirit of the original ideas and concepts. We are then able to share the concepts learned as if we were the originator of the concept.

FOLLOWING COMES AT A PRICE

> *If anyone comes to Me and does not hate his father and mother, wife and children, brothers and sisters, yes, and his own life also, he cannot be My disciple. And whoever does not bear his cross and come after Me cannot be My disciple. (Luke 14:26-27)*

To the above text, most of us would say something like this, *"Jesus, You are good and doing mighty things but that is my family."* Why would we say that? Because we are used to putting family before others. Putting family before others is not necessarily a bad thing, until it cost you a great deal.

Following requires a sacrifice of separation. Jesus is not asking us to hate our family, He is simply asking us to separate from them. God's desire for us is to trade our traditions, culture, beliefs and become embedded in the culture of the Kingdom of

Heaven. Our traditions should no longer be our go to, but the Kingdom of Heaven. Jesus is telling us to choose the kingdom ways above our own:

> *But seek first the kingdom of God and His righteousness, and all these things shall be added to you. (Matthew 6:33).*

Accept His will above our own will, our family's will, even above the will of our spouses.

Jesus is not saying we ought to hate our family or the world. That would not be true to His character, which is love. What He is saying, in my humble opinion, is that if it comes down to them, even with our own lives, we must choose Him above everything else. This is hard to understand, unless one can fully grasp what it means to be a disciple and sold out for the Kingdom of God.

BECOME LIKE THE TEACHER

> *A disciple is not above his teacher, but everyone who is perfectly trained will be like his teacher. (Luke 6:40).*

This is our goal, to become like our teacher and Lord, who is Jesus Christ. In the Jewish tradition, as a disciple, young men would leave their parent's home to travel and stay with their teacher for a period to learn his ways. They would eat, sleep, and drink the philosophy, concepts and knowledge that came from their teacher. The teacher was law when it came to ideas and opinion. The student had to submit his opinions and philosophies to the ideas and teachings of the teacher. The student didn't stop thinking for themselves, but they would begin to question the lesson, and in questioning the lesson, it allowed the teacher an opportunity to make it plain. The student's questions indicated to the teacher what needed to be explained or illustrated further so the student would get it. There is nothing wrong with questioning the teacher, if the goal is to understand the lesson. We need to release our ways and take on God's ways. Seek first the Kingdom of heaven and its ways and everything else will be added to you. We must be willing to forgo our ideas and let His ideas be true. Let God be true and every man a liar. *(See Romans 3:1-4).*

It was the goal of the student to get to know the teacher and his ways so in depth that when the student spoke, he sounded like the teacher. Anyone who knew the teacher would quickly be able to identify the teacher's students.

Modern Discipleship

It is my conviction that we are required to share what we know with others at some point in time. It may not be today, but some day we will be required to give an account of what we know to someone else. When the time comes, we should do it willingly and with a heart of gratitude.

For a disciple, it is less about what you know. We can possess all the knowledge and information of Google, and the internet, but if we do not allow this information to benefit others and ourselves, it is useless data. What we have learned and who we claim to the world we are, should be witnessed as well as heard.

We must be able to take what we have learned and put that into our life, demonstrating it to the world through our words and by how we live daily. Our knowledge must become wisdom. If all we know is in our heads and nothing has spilled over into our lives, we cannot be true disciples of Christ. What kind of witness for Christ can we be, if we do not take what we have learned and apply it in every area of our lives, not just the "Church" areas? For us to reach the lost, they must see the light in us.

People don't care what you know or who you know, until they know and can feel that you care about them. Take an example from your own life. We spend so little time with people that we feel do not care about us. People have to feel and see that we care, not just with words of service, but acts of service.

As a disciple, we should be willing to get our hands dirty. My grandfather used to say, *"You can't learn anything by just reading books. At some point you have to put into practice what you read."*

Do what you know to do, then consider what you do not know. Use what you know and do something with it. We will never know everything, and what we do not know, we do not know. Not knowing is no excuse for not doing. When we use what we know, someone will come alongside us and share what they know, and that will shed light on what we did not know.

We are so limited in our knowledge, and yet we act as if it takes a lot of education and knowledge to do what is helpful, beneficial, loving, kind and right.

EXPORT WHAT WE GROW

My grandmother would say, *"You can't get blood from a turnip."* I was always baffled by that saying, until the spirit behind the words hit me. No matter how hard we desire something, people can only give us what they have. The turnip does not bleed no matter how hard we press it.

Discipleship requires discipline and is an act of following with the hope of producing a better result over time. Discipline is another word for self-control. We should have control over ourselves regarding how we respond and react in "every" situation that we face daily.

We can always make a choice. You always have a choice. There is no able-bodied, adult person without a choice. We have the choice to go along with, stand against, retreat, quit, fight, and or do nothing. To be disciplined is to live a balanced life and that is a matter of choice. We need to choose to be disciplined in all areas of our lives. Our duty is to learn how to master ourselves, or at least understand ourselves to the point where we can explain when asked, *"Why did you do that when you could have easily done this."*

If God wanted us all to be the same, He would have made us the same. If He did not want us to have choice, He could have made us robots, not humans. As human beings, we have choices and each choice helps to shape us into the person we are or will become in a future moment.

CHOICES JUST ARE

Choices are not bad or good; they are options. The identifiers of good or bad is based on the outcome of the choice. We can increase our creative problem-solving skill, by not assigning good or bad to an option, but instead, looking at the options as what they are; an option, then run the outcome as desirable or undesirable, not good or bad.

Learning this skill will help us give critical thought to our choices, allowing us to see that even though the options are not all favorable, we still have choices that are more favorable. When we look at a choice as good or bad, we can assume that we don't have a choice because all the perceived results look bad.

We should think critically; think of all the results as you would a number scale, 1 being the most desirable result and 10 being the least desirable one.

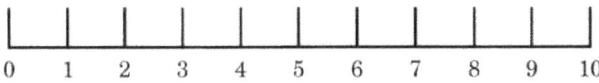

Once we have done this, then we should consider our options with the scale in mind. Which option will get us closer to our desired result? It will not change the options, but it will provide us with some options that we may not have considered before. Start with the desired outcome in mind, and then we can work backwards.

If we think **pre-action**, how will that action affect my desired result? Once we have begun to take steps, we need to think **in-action;** is this action putting me closer or further away from my desired outcome? Once we have completed a step, we need to think **post-action;** was this the best method, choice or decision? We must always ask ourselves, *"Could I have made a better choice?"* by looking at where we are after an action in relation to our desired outcome. This is how we learn from the journey; we question the steps, choices and decisions made before, during and after, always asking, *"Am I on or off course?"*

CHOICES AND DECISIONS ARE NOT THE SAME

Choices and decisions are not the same. Choices require the act of selecting what is preferred by separation or elimination. In making a choice we are always actively seeking that which is preferred; the better of the options. A decision is based on the root word 'decide,' which means to come to a definite conclusion or opinion. In deciding, you have fastened your mind on a conclusion. Therefore, our mind turns to that conclusion and responds accordingly.

Not every choice will get us our desired outcome. There are several reasons for this. One reason to consider is that we make a decision instead of making a conscience choice. For **Example, a friend inquires, "What are you doing this Saturday?" You decide to go grocery shopping, so you respond that you are going to the grocery store.** You decided that there are no options to consider. You decided that you are going to the grocery store on Saturday. There was nothing to consider, no options to choose from. Now imagine in that same conversation the person tosses in an option, for example, "I was wondering, because I have these two tickets to see your favorite group at this place on Saturday, would you like to go." You now have an option and you can consider the options, and then choose what is preferred.

That is how you make a choice. There are usually options to consider. Deciding does not mean that options are always present. When we learn how to make well considered choices, then we will develop a thought process that will lead us to carefully consider our decisions.

BALANCE IN EVERYTHING

Being imbalanced is to overindulge in any action, thought, or activity. Therefore, we have addicts and chronic criminal activity. Those folks have overindulged in an action, thought or activity that produced a habit and those habits produce their lifestyles. Telling a lie does not make you a liar, it makes you a person who has lied. There is a huge difference between someone who has stolen and a career thief, and someone who has lied and a liar. The main but not so obvious difference is the heart of the person. An overindulgence or a consistently repetitive behavior of such nature will make one of those things into a lifestyle or a way of being.

Think about it this way: thought + action + time spent doing = habit.

For us to form a habit we must do something overtime. No one acts without first having a thought. Conscious or subconscious, either way we had a thought to take an action. Some of us have formed habits to which the thought has moved into a rut, rail, or track zone. Even those ruts, rails, or tracks started with a simple thought. Stephen R. Covey who wrote "The Seven Habits of Highly Effective People" says, *"Sow a thought, reap an action; sow an action, reap a habit; sow a habit, reap a character; sow a character, reap a destiny."*

WE MUST BE DISCIPLINED

As a disciple, we must be disciplined in our actions and thoughts. Let us take a deeper look at three areas that will lead to a disciplined life:

1. **Thoughts** *(inner ideas or self-talk)*
2. **Speech** *(deliberate outer talk)*
3. **Action** *(what we do)*

Thoughts produce life, so as a man believes in his heart, so he will become:

> *For as he thinks in his heart, so is he. "Eat and drink!" he says to you, but his heart is not with you. (Proverbs 23:7).*

The question arises, what is the heart of man? Surely the heart is not just the internal organ that pumps blood to the body. I would like to suggest that the heart is the inner man, your soul. The heart is the internal, unseen part of a person that makes you who you are; your true self.

This has nothing to do with the body, but everything to do with the mind, will, and emotions. If our soul is dark, we will be dark. If our mind, will, and emotions are dark, we will be dark and people who meet us will see the darkness. Therefore, the heart is our emotions and desires that lie deep within our soul.

Follow Christ From Our Hearts

The contents of our heart cannot be hidden forever. We can hide our motive for only a short while but in the end, the contents of our heart will spill over into our life.

> *A good man out of the good treasure of his heart brings forth good; and an evil man out of the evil treasure of his heart brings forth evil. For out of the abundance of the heart his mouth speaks. (Luke 6:45)*

> *Keep your heart with all diligence, for out of it spring the issues of life. (Proverbs 4:23)*

Anyone who is around us for any length of time will be able to see what is in our heart. They will never know fully, but they will be able to see parts of our heart by listening to our words and seeing our actions in life. We must engage our heart, if we are to become true disciples of Christ. We must follow Christ from our hearts and not just our minds.

> *So he answered and said, "'You shall love the Lord your God with all your heart, with all your soul, with all your strength, and with all your mind,' and 'your neighbor as yourself.'" (Luke 10:27)*

To follow Christ, we must give Him our whole mind, and not just a part of it. To do this, we must learn to think with our whole mind, taking inventory of what comes in, what stays and what goes out. If we do not take *"every thought into captivity to the obedience of Christ"* (See 2 Corinthians 10:5), we will replicate destructive thoughts repeatedly, and we will think it is normal.

LIFE WILL PROVIDE OPPORTUNITIES FOR CHANGE

If your mind is set to a particular way of thinking, it is closed to new possibilities of being. Thinking with the whole mind is the act of examining every thought.

Life will provide many opportunities for change and growth but a person whose mind is locked will not see them. A locked mind will settle into a non-productive state. It will only react to ideas that already exist. It will not produce a new thought, idea, or process. In this state of mind, most people will go into a fierce defense of their stale ideas, beliefs, and processes. They are usually the ones who never want anything to change, and if it does, they want it to be so much like it was that the change is non-effective. This state of mind is what continues to keep good ideas from being great ideas. A good idea is something that can make a difference for a few. A great idea is something that will make a difference for many. So, what can we do if we are in this state of mind?

CHALLENGE ALL YOUR THOUGHTS

Locate a good place to start your internal research, but do not stop there. You may think you have hit the nail on the head, but dig deeper, seek more, test the answers and question your ideas.

Normally, when we are on an internal search, the first answer is usually just the beginning; all the mass and meat lie beneath the surface. Time, persistence, and patience will help us uncover the reasons we allowed our mind to slip into a neutral state. Once we have found the answer to our why, we will begin to challenge all our thoughts. When the old mind set reappears, ask these questions:

- Why am I thinking this way?

- Why do I trust this information?

- What about this thought? Could it be self-destructive?

- Does this thought help or hurt me?

Note, this will not happen overnight since our mind did not go into neutral overnight. Our mind has developed a very poor habit and we will have to purposefully develop a productive habit one thought at a time. Let it work its way out, and it will work its way out. Time and persistence are the key ingredients to it working its way out.

Take the time to listen, think and reflect. Learning to think in detail will appear to be long and drawn out in the early stages. Once we have developed this skill, it will take us far less time to think in detail. Snap decisions is a sure-fire way of knowing if we are in a state of reactive responding versus proactive thinking.

Here's a caution: Always look out for automatic thinking patterns where you just make snap judgments based on experiences only, never taking into consideration the new information presented. These are moments when you say, *"I have been there and done that"* or *"This will never work."* Instead, ask *"How"* so you can stay open to other options.

There is a time and place for other kinds of thought processes. We will discuss a type of reactive thinking in another chapter. Reactive thinking has killed many dreams, cut off new business ventures and destroyed many souls. We must check our thoughts at the door, making sure only the ones that are beneficial to our mental forest are the ones we allow to enter. All thoughts must be captured and put under guard so they cannot destroy the eco-system of our mental forest (mind). By not exercising our minds to move beyond what is present, the knowledge we have gained, or what we think we know and understand, become stale, stiffed necked and a poor example of Christ. We fail as a disciple, if we do not allow the Holy Spirit to work in our minds.

Think Of The Mind As A Radio

God did not make us bad, depressed, self-loathing and full of fear. God made us good, but we have become something other than what God made us to be. We did it, not God, by allowing ourselves to fall into the trap of not taking every thought captive.

Think of the mind as a radio and thoughts as stations. The mind processes information broadcasted through the air, but because it was broadcasted does not mean you have to tune in to it. You have the right and a duty to question everything that comes to your mind. **Why am I thinking this way? What purpose does this type of thinking serve? Who benefits from me thinking in this manner? How can I change this thought?**

TEND TO YOUR FOREST DAILY

We must learn to use our whole mind to think, because every thought is a seed. The more time we allow the past to infiltrate our minds without addressing the thoughts, the more power our minds have to determine whether the harvest is going to be productive or destructive. If a thought is a seed, then think of the mind as an eco-system or forest of sorts. It is our duty to make sure that what grows is beneficial to the overall health and life of the forest. Anything that enters the forest needs validation to ensure that it is in alignment with the overall goal of the forest's health, wealth, and purpose.

We must tend to our forest daily, ensuring that we are not allowing foreign, destructive thoughts to grow in our forest. Any idea or thought that is good today may not be good tomorrow. Therefore, we must take every thought captive and validate it against the overall health and direction of the mental forest. In essence, how do our thoughts line up with the word of God?

If we want physical fitness, we cannot allow the thought seed of laziness to grow or it will diminish our overall health. We thought and spoke our present life into existence. We may assume we did not think of poverty, heartache, pain, sickness, and any other negative situations we may have found ourselves involved in. We are usually the first to say, *"This is not my fault."* That may be true in some rare cases, but in most cases, our thoughts are at fault. We are what we think.

A man can build a skyscraper because he thought about it. Everything we see and experience in life today was just a thought in someone's mental forest. If you nurse the thought, it grows. Once the thoughts grow into a reality, they are ripe for harvesting from the unseen world and planted into the seen world. The unseen world of the mental forest is our imagination, our thinking center, our mind or the inner man. The material world begins in the unseen, and once it has matured, it becomes seen.

All we see in the world today that is good and profitable exists because someone was diligent, intentional, and purposefully tending to his or her mental forest. What are you allowing to grow in your mental forest that will solve the issues of life? Alternatively, what are you allowing to grow that will kill you and your mental forest all together?

Socrates once said he, "*...could not teach a man anything but only provoke him to think.*" I believe this to be a true statement. We cannot teach, only provoke one another to think. A thought unchecked is a time bomb waiting to explode. We must examine our thoughts so we can produce the life we want and not only accept the life we see.

Most of us are in our current situations by thoughts. Our thoughts have produced something that has snared us, propelled us, or stopped us from moving forward. We have become undisciplined in our thoughts, so we live an undisciplined life.

What does all this have to do with discipleship? If you don't understand how you are made and why Jesus is the perfect example, you will fall short of your call. Jesus did not call the elite to follow Him; He called the unique, the bold and the one's most would consider outcast and unworthy.

WHAT WE SAY DOES MATTER

What we think produces what we say; what we say produces what comes into our lives. The next area we must master or be fully aware of is how our speech, both internally and externally, works. What we say does matter.

We have heard the saying, *"Sticks and stones may break my bones, but words will never hurt me."* Our parents taught us that to guard our emotions against mean-spirited, foul mouth people who would spout nasty, negative, and demeaning comments. Truth is, words do and will hurt. It is not only someone else's words that can hurt, but our own when it is in agreement with theirs. Therefore, sticks and stones will break your bones and words can hurt you, but only if you are in agreement.

We speak for others to hear; we listen to understand, and we act to execute what was spoken. Speech can be defined as active sound production, which translates into a pattern that produces language. This language formed by words communicate ideas, concepts, and emotions to ourselves or another person who understands the language of speech. We must always define words and concepts based on what they mean to us, so we can convey how we want them understood by others. Speech produces life. Everything we see is manifested by words spoken, and that creates existence.

> *In the beginning was the Word, and the Word was with God, and the Word was God. He was in the beginning with God. All things were made through Him, and without Him nothing was made that was made. In Him was life, and the life was the light of men. And the light shines in the darkness, and the darkness did not comprehend it. There was a man sent from God, whose name was John. This man came for a witness, to bear witness of the Light, that all through him might believe. He was not that Light, but was sent to bear witness of that Light. That was the true Light which gives light to every man coming into the world. He was in the world, and the world was made through Him, and the world did not know Him. He came to His own, and His own did not receive Him. But as many as received Him, to them He gave the right to become children of God, to those who believe in His name: who were born, not of blood, nor of the will of the flesh, nor of the will of man, but of God. And the Word became flesh and dwelt among us, and we beheld His glory, the glory as of the only begotten of the Father, full of grace and truth. (John 1:1-14)*

The Universe was spoken into existence by Jesus. In the same way Jesus spoke the universe into being, we have the same ability to speak our life into being. We are the product of someone speaking about us, to us and over us.

When a mother desires to bear children, the first thing she does is think about having children, then she speaks about having them. Someone spoke about you, and then someone spoke to you. Parents have a little practice where they speak to their little babies while they are in the stomach. Once they are born, they speak about them, telling friends, neighbors or anyone who will listen about their new bundle of joy.

Someone is always speaking to us, about us or over us. When we were children, those words shaped us, hurt us, healed us, pushed us, pulled us, helped us and caused us emotional harm. Nonetheless, the words that we speak affect us. We became by our speech. Now that we are adults, we can either sit and repeat those words or we can stop, examine, validate, or remove those words. The tongue has the power to set the world ablaze or douse the flames of despair with hope-filled words. We must control our speech, if we desire to live a disciplined and balanced life.

THE ART OF THE TONGUE

The tongue can paint a world of beauty,

Or a pit of terror, filled with gloomy days.

It can build up self-esteem, or slowly burn it away.

It can bring hope to the hopeless, and inspiration to the weak.

So, watch your words, for what you intend,

May not be what you speak.

Speech is a job, and the tongue the tool.

Masterpieces of growth in the hands of wisdom,

Destruction in the hands of a fool.

We must control what we say to others and to ourselves. Once words are infused into our speech, they will plant seeds into the listener that we do not desire most of the time. We are the first person to hear those words, so when we think we are cursing someone out by using words to harm another person, we are harming our self. Be mindful of your words at all times. The Bible teaches that we will give an account for every idle word spoken:

> *But I say to you that for every idle word men may speak, they will give account of it in the day of judgment. (Matthew 12:36).*

SPEAK WITH PURPOSE

Speak with purpose, not from pain. Sometimes we want to provoke a person to action, so we speak on purpose via persuasive, emotional speech. Other times we want to relay the pain we are experiencing, so emotional speech is a useful tool then. That kind of speech is acceptable under those circumstances, but otherwise, we end up hitting many innocent people with words of death. Think of words as a meal that we are feeding to someone. A good meal is seasoned properly, not too much or too little, but just right.

When we open our mouths to *"serve"* that meal, we must be very mindful of the *"seasoning"* we choose to infuse into that meal. Will we *"serve"* a meal that heals and soothes or one that causes pain and ultimately kill the hearer? Death to the physical body is assured at some point, but there is another type of death which is not physical. The worst kind of death is one that wounds or kills a person's spirit. This kind of death will lead to multiple deaths.

It is believed that hurting people hurt people. They are like the walking dead. These individuals are people who have died inside; their hope is lost. They no longer have a vision (the art of dreaming), trust, or belief in the impossible. They have become dream assassins, hope stealers and life takers. People who have lost hope are truly the most miserable.

We destroy worlds by what we say, so let us learn to manage, monitor and master our speech. When we say something negative, we are not only hurting the person we are directing the words toward, but we are hurting ourselves as well.

I always found it interesting that 'words' and 'sword' have the same letters; the only difference is where the "s" is positioned. We call the Word of God our sword. Therefore, our words are our sword. We use them to protect, project or reject ideas and concepts that come against the knowledge and the truth of Jesus as the Christ and the only One begotten of the Father. We use our words to state, proclaim and name situations. We have so much power in our words.

YOUR WORDS, YOUR SWORD

The sword, which you thought was going to strike down your enemy, may be the same sword that you stumble over and kill yourself. Be mindful that your sword hits the intended target. When we speak, we are the first ones to hear our words and they are laced with power. They can build or kill, and you decide the outcome.

When we set out to do harm with our words to others, we destroy ourselves in the process because we will reap what we sow. Speech is always a seed. We will be judged by every idle word we speak. We are responsible for every word that comes out of our mouths. We must take inventory of our harvest and see what words (seeds) we can tie back to our current situation.

I used to tell my kids when they were younger, *"Never say what you do not want to live."* This led to confusion as they got older. They thought I was telling them not to share what they were thinking and feeling. It was not easy trying to explain what I meant to a 6 and 8-year-old, mainly because I was not emotionally tuned or seeking to understand them. I was more focused on getting the concepts into them. I did not employ the number one rule of relationship building, *"People don't care how much you know, until they know how much you care."* Children are no different; they need to feel that you care, before you can give them what you know. So, my words fell on deaf ears, hearts and minds. I have since explained what I meant and apologized to them for my harsh approach to the situation. They felt for many years that I had no feeling, no emotions.

We must own our mistakes. We cannot expect people to let that infraction go so easily. When we own it, we create an opportunity to begin again. At the time, I did not own my mistakes, so my speech was not full of compassion that comes from a place of love and understanding. If you are not able to season your words with the salt of love, then you may need to examine further your reason for saying, thinking, and doing.

Love must be the filter through which every word flow, if we are to reach the intended goal of mutual understanding. We must be mindful of what fills our minds, if we want our words to work for and not against us.

WORDS

I dance on paper stages.

I am an illustration on the canvass of the mind.

I bring tears to the hearts of conscience

And joy to the soul of thought.

I start with little momentum but conclude with dramatic endings.

I am a tease to the drama of romance and suspense to the mysteries of comprehension.

I evade the truth of reality with fictitious tales.

I tempt the realm of imagination with slanted phrases.

I lie with truth but stand with fantasy.

I aggravate the grounds of belief with different versions of reality.

I can only be seen through the mind's eye.

I can only be heard through the voice of imagination.

SPEECH FROM ONE GENERATION TO THE NEXT

Most traditions are passed on through speech from one generation to the next. Therefore, our speech developed prior to handwriting. Speech has the power to shape us in ways that other forms of communication cannot. We could repeat faster and more accurately song lyrics versus reading the same lyrics. Our speech is driven by our thoughts and what we choose to talk about drives what we think; they are all part of our cognitive system.

The cognitive system is the thought center of a person, and it is where we receive and relay information. Information is not the only thing that goes into this system, but it is the main function that drives the system.

MASTER YOUR THOUGHTS

If everything we do starts with what we think and what we speak gives life to our thoughts, then we can conclude that our actions or the way in which we live is based on our thoughts.

If we are to master our behavior, we must first master our speech both internally and externally. This is the only way we can ever truly alter the way we act. We are not acting out, we are acting in. We are slaves to our thought life, and we cannot resist but carry out what we think the most. If we agree to these concepts, then we can assume one more thing as it relates to discipline. The way we view the world will drive what and how we think. We act on who we think we are, not what we see in others.

Life is nothing but a game that is played first in the mind and then we act. We act based on the mental moves that first start in the mind. Since we need to be a disciple of Christ, we must first adapt the mind of Christ. We can choose not to be a disciple and that is our free-will choice.

We must know how God thinks, so we can take the seeds He has provided through the reading of His Word and by forging a relationship with Him. We must plant the seeds we get from this practice in our mental forest, so they can grow into a harvest. The harvest will look like Christ perfected in Love. We will bear spiritual fruit:

> *But the fruit of the Spirit is love, joy, peace, longsuffering, kindness, goodness, faithfulness, gentleness, self-control. Against such there is no law. (Galatians 5:22-23).*

The tree of love will bear joy, peace, longsuffering, gentleness, goodness, faith, meekness, and temperance (self-control). It is imperative that we understand and agree that everything we do begins within us based on a thought. We move based on thoughts, not right nor wrong, but thoughts of right and wrong. We are a part of the game, some willing and others reluctant, but at the end of the day, we are part of the game.

> *Then He spoke many things to them in parables, saying: "Behold, a sower went out to sow. And as he sowed, some seed fell by the wayside; and the birds came and devoured them. Some fell on stony places, where they did not have much earth; and they immediately sprang up because they had no depth of earth. But when the sun was up they were scorched, and because they had no root they withered away. And some fell among thorns, and the thorns sprang up and choked them. But others fell on good ground and yielded a crop: some a hundredfold, some sixty, some thirty. He who has ears to hear, let him hear!" (Matthew 13:3-9).*

GOD GIVEN SEEDS

God created a system and that system works the same for everyone. Seed time and harvest is a system. All seeds that come from God are good, and oftentimes they come as thoughts, which produces a good harvest over time. The thought seed is the beginning for all that exist, and these seeds must be planted in fertile ground. *What is fertile ground?* Fertile ground is where the mental forest is cultivated, negativity and evil thoughts are recognized and quickly discarded, and it is where every thought is taken captive. It is where the fruits of the Spirit reign and grow in abundance.

In addition, fertile ground is where the mind is open to the leading of the Holy Spirit, the desire to become more like Christ and the will to be like Him and to obey His word are present. To be fertile ground is to be open to new ideas that the Holy Spirit deposits. These ideas must be tested to prove them good and from God. God means you no harm. It is His will that you prosper and be in good health.

> *"I say this because I know the plans that I have for you." This message is from the Lord. "I have good plans for you. I don't plan to hurt you. I plan to give you hope and a good future. Then you will call my name. You will come to me and pray to me, and I will listen to you. You will search for me, and when you search for me with all your heart, you will find me." (Jeremiah 29:11-13 - ERV).*

God is always trying to seed our garden with His seeds. One seeks to destroy those good and God-given seeds. This is the enemy, the devil, evil or any idea that comes up against the Word of truth. The devil is always working to cast doubt on the Word of God in our mind. He will use anything at his disposal to do this. He is the god of this world so the whole world is at his disposal. The enemy, the devil, is a liar and the father of lies. Nothing he says is true. Even if it sounds true, if the devil said it, it is a lie. To help you combat his attacks, the word of God has given us some tactics to help us cultivate a garden that is full of love, hope, faith, peace and joy.

> *Finally, brethren, whatever things are true, whatever things are noble, whatever things are just, whatever things are pure, whatever things are lovely, whatever things are of good report, if there is any virtue and if there is anything praiseworthy—meditate on these things. (Philippians 4:8).*

We choose what we think about. We make choices on what we let live, die and grow in our mental forest. There is a common enemy, and he is hell bent on destroying us. Yes, the devil is a common enemy, but he is not the enemy I am speaking of here only. I am talking about the enemy of passivity, the one that thrives when we refuse to choose or decide. The devil is an enemy that comes in when we are tired and refuse to make a choice to get moving. His goal is to kill, steal and destroy (See John 10:10).

We are under constant attack and some of us are in a battle at this very moment with passivity. We allow him to do whatever he likes. We accept every thought seed as an identity verifier instead of verifying the idea to see if it aligns with the truth. We go along with inaction and call it making peace. Remember, the devil will use whatever is at his disposal. The fact that you are acting passive, he will use passivity to destroy you and your future.

WE ARE IN A BATTLE

We are in a battle and to win we must get up and fight, but not with knives, guns, and baseball bats. We must fight with knowledge and wisdom, which we gain once we have applied God's truths to our lives. Our weapons for this battle must be love, kindness, and self-control. We must fight with pureness of thought. We must fight with purpose. We must think, speak, and do everything with purpose. We cannot be passive in any area, if we want to succeed in every area. The enemy is about the destruction of our inner world. He came to steal, kill, and destroy your mental forest.

> *The thief does not come except to steal, and to kill, and to destroy. I have come that they may have life, and that they may have it more abundantly. (John 10:10).*

The devil knows and understands that if he can get you out of balance in any area of life, he can destroy you. Passiveness and being overly ambitious creates imbalance. We can do something too much. If we reach that point of too much, we will find that we have lost our balance and our way.

In the beginning stages of learning martial arts, the focus is on your stance (form). To have a strong fighting stance, you must first have good balance. This is true in real fights as well as a mental one. We must have balance, if we are going to be the victor in any fight, but this is not the only thing you need. It is the foundation for which we can build our victories. Balance requires discipline, discipline requires practice, and practice requires patience.

We must understand that God created everything and in Him we exist. He is our foundation of true balance.

> *For by Him all things were created that are in heaven and that are on earth, visible and invisible, whether thrones or dominions or principalities or powers. All things were created through Him and for Him. And He is before all things, and in Him all things consist. (Colossians 1:16-17)*

To be a follower of Christ, we must be as disciplined as He was when He was going to the cross. It was not an easy task for Christ. He was in the Garden of Gethsemane with His disciples, and He asked them to come and pray with Him. He was going through a heavy ordeal and was feeling the weight of His choice to die for the sin-filled world. His journey came down to that one moment: He knew He was going to die. Let us hear what He had to say about the situation:

Then Jesus came with them to a place called Gethsemane, and said to the disciples, "Sit here while I go and pray over there." And He took with Him Peter and the two sons of Zebedee, and He began to be sorrowful and deeply distressed. Then He said to them, "My soul is exceedingly sorrowful, even to death. Stay here and watch with Me." He went a little farther and fell on His face, and prayed, saying, "O My Father, if it is possible, let this cup pass from Me; nevertheless, not as I will, but as You will." Then He came to the disciples and found them sleeping, and said to Peter, "What! Could you not watch with Me one hour? Watch and pray, lest you enter into temptation. The spirit indeed is willing, but the flesh is weak." Again, a second time, He went away and prayed, saying, "O My Father, if this cup cannot pass away from Me unless I drink it, Your will be done." (Matthew 26:36-42).

Jesus was in a world of hurt. He was in a battle. He knew He had to yield His will to the Father's will, if He was going to finish the race. Here is where the rubber meets the road. Jesus wanted to avoid the cross, but Christ desired the cross. Jesus wanted the pain to stop, but Christ welcomed the pain because He knew by every stripe we would be healed. Jesus wanted to find another way, but Christ knew it was the only way.

BECOME ONE WITH YOUR TWO

Jesus and Christ were two but one. You will have to become one with your two. You must let the mind of Christ rule in you and not allow the mind of comfort and passiveness rule over your "doing." The comfort that I am speaking of is not a comfort of rest; the comfort I am speaking of is laziness, procrastination and passivity. We should rest and enjoy life, but we should not look to avoid work just so we can be comfortable.

> *For what if some did not believe? Will their unbelief make the faithfulness of God without effect? Certainly not! Indeed, let God be true but every man a liar. As it is written: "That You may be justified in Your words, and may overcome when You are judged." (Romans 3:3-4)*

Take a stand with the Christ and let the desire to be more like Him live in you so you can conquer the need for a comfortable existence. I am not saying that you will not have comfort, because you will. I am saying do not look to be comfortable as you journey.

We must embrace our cross and let go of our idea that the journey must be comfortable. To be a disciple, we must be willing to endure the cross that Jesus so wanted to avoid but Christ embraced. When we look for comfort, we lose sight of the journey and the discipline needed to finish the race. Looking for comfort takes our eyes off the prize. We can become distracted and lose focus of the goal. The goal is, and should always be, to fulfill the will of God, not our will, but the Father's.

In the beginning of any type of change, there will be some form of discomfort. We can only hope that we finish the journey before our time ends. Jesus lived thirty-three years on this earth, and in that time, He completed what He came to do. Some of us have lived twice that and have not begun the journey of fulfillment. We have a part to play, and if we are ever going to live up to our purpose and full potential, we must discipline ourselves. May I suggest that we become a follower of the living God through the process of being a disciple of Christ. He came that we may have life, and have it more abundantly, but we will never have what He promised if we do not get onboard the disciple-ship.

STOP PRETENDING

Do not let another moment past without you accepting this truth. We must get on board and lay down every weight that comes against us to prevent us from having discipline. If we truly want to be successful at anything, we will need to develop a disciplined mind. If we want to build a house, a business, or a life, it requires discipline. So, stop pretending we do not need to live a disciplined life and let us take the next step. We can't do this alone, so let us start with getting to know Jesus the Christ. Make Him our Team Captain, Coach and Star Player. With

Jesus on our team, and us on His, this life is a guaranteed victory.

PRAYER

Lord, I am a sinner and I cannot live this life without You. I have fallen short of Your glory and I accept Jesus, Your Son, as my Redeemer, Provider, Life-Giver, Lord and Savior. Jesus, I make You head of my life. I no longer want to do life without You. Teach me Your ways. I want to be a disciple of You, the Lord of lords and King of kings. You are the most-high God. I surrender all to You and for You. I desire Your way and not my way, Your truth and not the lies of the world. I no longer want to do it my way. Lord have Your way in my life, in Jesus name I pray. Amen.

If that was the first time you ever prayed this prayer, I would like to be the first to welcome you to the family, the winning team. I encourage you to find a body of like-minded people you can fellowship with. Life is a team sport, so find a place you can go practice and become part of a community of people who are living and walking with Christ.

CHAPTER 5 OUTRO

To do anything of great value requires discipline. To be a professional or expert at a task, one must spend 10,000 hours in that task in the form of practice. That requires discipline of mind, time and body.

We have a great example in Christ Jesus. He made us in His image. We also have the Spirit of the Living God. Our spirit is ready to move ahead in victory, but often our flesh is weak and stuck in comfort and passivity. Don't lose your way because you have become out of balance. Lean into and on the Lord and let Him show you how to live this life in discipline.

CHAPTER 5 TAKE AWAY

1. Discipleship requires discipline.

2. Discipline is about having balance in all areas.

3. Life, change and progress is uncomfortable so get comfortable being uncomfortable or you will fall into the trap of passivity.

4. Passivity is the enemy to all progress. Learn to act with conviction and discipline to overcome the pull of being passive.

Chapter 6

Stewardship: Managing Our Resources

The Ship called Steward just docked at Port Opportunity, right next to Port Temptation. Port Temptation looks just like you would imagine every great port to look like. There is free admission and all you must give is your time, mind, and emotions. Every thought of "I want" would be granted but the truth is, Port Temptation is a ploy, and a deeply calculated scheme to break your diligence of serving and focusing all you have on the mighty "we" and place it only on the "ME." Port Temptation is a deep hole filled with falsehoods, fulfillment of nothing, broken heartedness, and despair.

On the other side sits this old worn Port called Opportunity. It doesn't look like much and the price to enter is high, and you must work, it if you ever want it to thrive. It is where blessings hide, like treasure beneath stones of discipline, service, and stewardship. At that Port, you are not the focus and never will be. You must help one another, if you want to receive the wealth hidden within Port Opportunity. Port Opportunity is not for the weak, but the meek, the ones who have a heart that is tender and not focused on the mighty "ME." To board Port Opportunity, you must be willing to sacrifice your seat, drop to your knees and give to all in need. I met Jesus at Port Opportunity. He was standing there telling all who was heavy laden to come to Him and He would give us a life filled with more in exchange for our sinful natures, dirtiness, and life of labor and chore. Jesus said, *"Give me your punishment, that you may live. I am the truth, the way, the life, and love; and this love to you I will give, so an abundant life you can live."*

Jesus is the great Steward who came and fulfilled what God told Him to do in His thirty-three years on earth. He was looking for someone, anyone, who was willing to sacrifice for the next person as He did. He was looking for grown people to come to Him with expectancy like little kids, eyes wide, hearts wide and hope flowing from them like water from ice cubes on a hot summer day. Port Opportunity is the place I learned stewardship. Jesus was that opportunity.

I learned that it was not about me. If I wanted to be free, I had to lose my life, drop my anger, and turn from strife. I learned that true power was in self-control. I learned to be a good steward of my mind, will, and emotions. I learned how to care for what was in my charge, even though I never really owned it. None of it was mine, it was His, and He gave me charge of it. It was on loan. He expects me to flourish and multiply. He ensured my victories. He shed His blood to wipe my sin of debt clean. All He asked is that I be a good steward over the new opportunity; the life He died to give me.

> *As each one has received a gift, minister it to one another, as good stewards of the manifold grace of God. (1 Peter 4:10).*

Here is the definition of **steward** from the Webster dictionary: *"One employed in a large household or estate to manage domestic concerns: A fiscal agent: an employee on a ship, airplane, bus, or train who manages the provisioning of food and attends to the passengers: one appointed to supervise the provision and distribution of food and drink in an institution: One who actively directs affairs: manager.*

Larry Burket wrote, *"When we surrender every area of our lives-- including our finances--to God, then we are free to trust Him to meet our needs. But if we would rather hold tightly to those things that we possess, then we find ourselves in bondage to those very things."*

Here is my definition of **steward:** *one who is fully aware of the items placed in his charge, knowing that they are not his to own, but are on loan to cherish as his, so that they are able to grow and become profitable. A good steward knows what he has charge over and is willing to stake his life on protecting it.*

Jesus was such a steward. He created everything but allowed us to work with Him in the enjoyment and maintenance of His creation. Rick Warren writes, *"At the end of your life on earth you will be evaluated and rewarded according to how well you handled what God entrusted to you."*

STEWARDSHIP OVER ALL

We have a great opportunity here. We have been given charge over the earth, and we have an opportunity to aid God in the running of the planet. What an awesome privilege and great responsibility we have as humans. God saw to it that we run the planet with Him, not without Him. Everything else is on loan, and the sooner we understand this, the better we will be on this journey.

Before we set off on any journey, it is a good practice to see what we have by taking an inventory of our resources, just to be sure we have what we need. We don't want to be lost or confused about what He wants. He left us a Comforter, a Guide, and a Teacher. He left His Holy Spirit as our greatest resource so we can be in constant contact with the Father and never lose sight of the goal.

A steward is a manager who can fully enjoy, or fully abuse, what is in his charge or care. We have full control over what Jesus has left in our care. We cannot be good stewards by shear nature. The Holy Spirit must teach us and then we follow the model that God has given us in Jesus Christ. If we are to steward as Jesus did, which is entirely possible, we must give our best at everything we do. We must treat our neighbor's house as if it was our own and take great care of it. We must treat the parks, and public places as if we spent the time and labor to build them.

A father is a steward. It is his duty to provide, protect and care for the house and for the family he created and accepted as his, which is a great honor. It is selfish and poor stewardship to not care and provide. Remembering that they are not ours to own but is on loan can be challenging.

The hardest part is letting go and returning the gifts, talents and even our families back to the Father. We are in control over something as precious as life, and when the time comes for us to release it, we often find it downright impossible to lay it at the altar of grace and mercy so that we can redeem it for an eternal one. Do not hold on to the perishable and refuse the imperishable. Your life is also on loan, so return it back to the Father so He can redeem it for all eternity.

When people talk about stewardship, it always leads to a conversation about money or finances, but that is just a part and not the main part. Therefore, I am going to give you my take on the fiscal part of stewardship. It is not yours, so give cheerfully and without looking for something in return. When we make an investment, we naturally look for a return. As a steward, you should invest in yourself and others with the hope of growing them and yourselves, and not look for a return.

As the modern church, we tithe with the expectation of receiving something in return. It is not a gift if we expect a return. I also believe that when we give an offering, we should give it with the full understanding that it was not ours in the first place.

He gave us the gift of life. The money we make is also a gift. We worked for it, but the breath of life we used was from the Father. I am not saying you should give all your money to the "Church," neither am I saying that you should only give to a church. I am saying that when, where and to whom you give; ensure you give it with a cheerful heart expecting nothing in return. It should be our pleasure to make sure the Father gets a return on His investment for providing us the breath of life. God doesn't really care what kind of house you live in, or what kind of car you drive. He cares if you have been a good steward and provided a return on His investment. He wants to know that we used all the gifts and talents He gave us for the betterment of the world. Did we sit on it and watch it waste? We have become lazy and fruitless, not being our best. We have settled for mediocrity and that is displeasing to the Father.

What House Has Your Heart? What Car Drives You?

You are here to flourish and give a return on the investment of Jesus's life that paid it all with the hope of redeeming us back to the Father. God gave you the position of steward over His creation. You did not work for this life, it was a gift. You did not work for His love, it was a gift. A good steward understands that one day he will have to answer for how he managed what he was given.

Robert J. Shiller writes, *"Finance is not merely about making money. Finance is about achieving our deep goals and protecting the fruits of our labor. It is about stewardship and therefore about achieving the good society."*

LOVE IS THE INVESTMENT

Give what was given so that the Father can receive a return on His investment. Love is the investment that the Father has given and out of His love for us, He gave His only begotten Son. Since He has invested His love in us, we must give love to others. Love is an action word and requires you to give up something; it requires you to move. If you love me, but do not give me the bare minimum, what type of love is that? God gave generously so we should do the same and give on purpose. If you have three cars and your brother has none, and if you claim to love your brother, and you see he needs transportation and God has blessed you with the ability to have three cars, why wouldn't you give to your brother who is in need?

GIVE YOUR BEST

You are not a good steward if you are not willing to give your best to make sure you have more than enough. So, when the opportunity presents itself, you have something to give. One must have an evil heart to see a need and have what it takes to fill that need and choose not to.

Money is a tool, like a hammer and a nail. Money can be used to build a better life for you, leave a legacy, and build your community. Money should not be hoarded, nor only be spent fast and furiously with no regards. Money should be used to make life better, solve a problem and help those who are less fortunate. Everything done with money should be for God's glory or else money becomes a god that serves our every whim and desire.

Most people stop themselves when it comes to giving. They refuse to give to someone who is not to their liking, but that is not our call. You will need to refer to the Holy Spirit on how, when, who and how much you should give at any given moment. If you invest what you have been given and get a return on that investment, you will have more than enough to give. As John Eczema rightly says, *"Transparency, honesty, kindness, good stewardship, even humor, work in businesses always."*

SELFISHNESS AND NOT SELFLESSNESS

The society in which the world operates is one of selfishness and not selflessness. We care more about our status in the eyes of men, so we are willing to spend, spend, and spend more than we have so we can appear to be more than we are. Most of us live above our means and complain when we cannot seem to get financial freedom. This action where we are taking from our future to satisfy our present, while we sip on regrets from the past, is a misuse of our finances. Afterwards, we complain about not having enough and needing more, but refuse to save. So, when trouble comes, we have nothing in store. Therefore, we work harder, longer, and climb ladders of success looking for relief when the answer is simple; become a good steward and live within your means. Manage the intake and the output of your resources. Stop living for the praise of others; instead, live for the applause of Jesus, the King of kings.

A good steward knows when to disperse and when to keep close, knowing what will bring the most return for their investment. Stewardship is just another word for manager. We are required to manage our resources. *What is a resource?* A resource is a skill, talent, gift, time, or an idea. It is what you have that you can leverage to make your life and the life of someone else better. God is not asking you to save the world, He already did that through Jesus Christ. He is not even asking you to give to everyone, but He is asking that you give your life to Him so He can show you how to get a return on His investment.

SHARE IT AND MAKE IT GROW

Warren Buffet is known worldwide to be a good investor. He built a huge fortune, investing some Thirty-Six Billion dollars. Imagine Warren coming to you and giving you access to all his wealth, with one caveat; you must let him show you how to invest it. This is what God has done. He has given us, as people, access to His fortune with one request; allow Him to show you how to care for it properly.

While you have it, enjoy it, share it and make it grow, so others can enjoy it as well. This is what God is asking us to do; be a good steward. In the process, you still get to enjoy the fortune. God gave us all, so we can have all, but to have all, He must be our all. God wants to be the steward (manager) of our soul, so we are safe from ourselves (our flesh).

God does not need anything; He has everything, but He wants to give us all He has. He wants to entrust His creation to us, but He knows we will only destroy it and ourselves if left to ourselves by ourselves. *How can we become a great steward?* We must yield to the leading of the Holy Spirit. We must invite Jesus into every part of our lives, no exceptions, and nothing is off limits.

We must give up control of what we think we want, so we can have what God has placed in us. There are countless books written on how to be a good manager/steward, but the fact of the matter is this, for us as humans who have been given life by God, the answer is simple; yield your will to His as well as read some of those countless books.

> *For I know the thoughts that I think toward you, says the Lord, thoughts of peace and not of evil, to give you a future and a hope. (Jeremiah 29:11).*

JESUS WAS AND IS OUR EXAMPLE

God is seeking someone, anyone, who will allow Him to be head of their life so He can bless them with what He has in store for them. Stop trying to do life alone. Jesus was and is our example so ask Him what to do with your gifts, skills, and talents. Seek Him for guidance in all things and this will make you a good steward, if you are willing to let go and obey Him in all.

GOD IS LOOKING FOR A FAITHFUL SERVANT

Then Peter said to Him, "Lord, do You speak this parable only to us, or to all people?" And the Lord said, "Who then is that faithful and wise steward, whom his master will make ruler over his household, to give them their portion of food in due season? Blessed is that servant whom his master will find so doing when he comes. Truly, I say to you that he will make him ruler over all that he has. But if that servant says in his heart, 'My master is delaying his coming,' and begins to beat the male and female servants, and to eat and drink and be drunk, the master of that servant will come on a day when he is not looking for him, and at an hour when he is not aware, and will cut him in two and appoint him his portion with the unbelievers. (Luke 12:41-46).

God is looking for a faithful servant who is just, diligent, and willing to work. This steward is what we need to become; someone who is willing to do right by all that is under our charge. We are not to be selfish, self-serving nor self-seeking if we want the benefit from what the Father has planned for a faithful servant.

All that you have is because God is. If there was no God, there would be no you. Jesus is the only way to the Father so listen to what Jesus is asking on behalf of us all:

> *"Father, I desire that they also whom You gave Me may be with Me where I am, that they may behold My glory which You have given Me; for You loved Me before the foundation of the world. O righteous Father! The world has not known You, but I have known You; and these have known that You sent Me. And I have declared to them Your name, and will declare it, that the love with which You loved Me may be in them, and I in them." (John 17:24-26).*

Jesus is essentially pleading for us to give Him our little in exchange for His much. He will exchange our filthy rags for His royal robe; and our broken perception of who we are for a full picture of who He created us to be. Will you accept the gift and let God Steward your life by the Holy Spirit and following the great Steward, Christ?

Chapter 6 Outro

We want to be a good steward and live a life that is full, but we constantly settle for what is. We squander our resources and let circumstances steward our lives. Turn over the reins to Jesus and allow Him full access to your life and you will have life more abundantly. This is the way we become a better steward. We must give up control of what we think we want, so we can have what God has placed in us.

There are countless books written on how to be a good manager/steward, but the fact of the matter is this, for us as humans who have been given life by God, the answer is simple; yield your will to His.

Chapter 6 Take Away

1. **Stewardship is just another word for manager.** We are required to manage our resources.

2. **A resource is a skill, talent, gift, time, or an idea.** It is what you have that you can leverage to make your life and the life of someone else better.

3. **Manage the intake and the output of your resources.** Stop living for the praise of others and instead live for the applause of Jesus, the King of kings.

CHAPTER 7

Partnership: Collaborating with God the Father through Jesus and Others

Contrary to popular culture and media, there is no such thing as a self-made man or woman. They need the aid, guidance, stewardship, friendship, relationship, leadership, fellowship and partnership of others to make it. We have some things by pure will power, but if we look closely, we will see that in the process, someone came along and gave us, at least, a word of encouragement.

Maybe that word/help came from an ad, a book or someone who just happened to cross our path. No matter how it came, there was another person who helped along the way. Nonetheless, I stand by my statement, no self-made man or woman exist or ever will. We need someone to help us navigate the waters of this journey called life.

CONNECTING WITH THE RIGHT PARTNERS

We need to partner with the right people at the right time for the completion of a goal/vision, with the right collaborates, i.e., the Holy Spirit and Jesus, who are our direct connection to God the Father. We have a great start for living a life of purpose and success, but we require more partners. God made us that way; we need other people. We were created to be in a relationship with Jesus. God the Father, in all His love and wisdom, decided to do one better; He decided to give us, who are broken, self-centered, with a sinful nature, the opportunity to collaborate with Him and His Son, Jesus the Christ, as part of the harvest process. We get the opportunity to be the body of the living God. An Unknown source wrote, *"Wanting a partner or the desire to be a partner is easy work, but the development of a partnership is a slow process, like ripening of a fruit."*

The Webster dictionary defines **Partnership** in the following manner: *the state of being a partner: participation; a legal relation existing between two or more persons contractually associated as joint principals in a business; the persons joined in a partnership; a relationship resembling a legal partnership and usually involving close cooperation between parties having specified and joint rights and responsibilities.*

Partnership is a compound word. Its root word is *partner* and here is how the Webster dictionary defines partner: *archaic: one that shares, partaker; one associated with another especially in an action: associate, colleague; either of two persons who dance together; one of two or more persons who play together in a game against an opposing side; a person with whom one shares an intimate relationship: one member of a couple; a member of a partnership especially in a business.*

Another Unknown source wrote, *"Just one great partnership with the right person at the right time can have an incredible impact on your life, business, and family success. Stay on the lookout for this great partnership because it can and will change your life."*

The quote above makes me think of Jesus as that one great partner. In this life we will meet so many people along the way, but how do we make use of the opportunity to become a part of their solution? We must be willing to walk with them that extra mile to see them to the end, or as far as we can go with them. Most of us do not take partnerships seriously; we look at them as **WIIFM** *(What's In It For Me?)*.

This may work in marketing or investing options, but it should not be the viewpoint when it comes to partnerships. We should look at what we can add to a partnership, so that all parties move ahead as a unit. We think "me" first, and who can blame us when the past one thousand years has been focused on you being what you want to be. Life is all about you, so you don't need a kind stranger to snap a pic; you just pull out your selfie stick and take the pic. This is a poor state of affairs when we rely more on systems, technology, and machines for the sole purpose of saying, "I don't need anyone to help me."

We Suffer From The Lack Of A Real Connection

Today, we have more ways to connect but we rarely have a human connection because we refuse to disconnect from our virtual world of fake friends and fake likes. How did we fall so far from the nature of humanity where we have so many social media apps online, but nothing for real time? What went wrong? We have become callous, self-righteous, self-focused, and self-centered. We are so full of self that we have no room or space for anyone else.

Why do we disconnect when there is no reason not to connect? We use text for face to face, emojis to convey how we feel, and leave a lot of room for mis-interpretation. We have become masters of shorthand text speech, but not able to share our thoughts with words. There is nothing wrong with utilizing technology as another means of communication, but if we use it in addition and not solely as a means, the rift in communication may be minimal. We have all this technology to help us stay connected, but we suffer from a lack of a real connection. We are lonely; in a world full of people who we cannot connect to.

When living calcifies, life is easier behind the screen than it is to participate openly and fearlessly. Life is not a spectator sport, it requires participation and getting dirty so we can help others.

We need exposure to other ideas that will challenge our ideas from people with a different background than ours. Once we are exposed to something different, our whole world is open to new possibilities. Exposure opens us to a new way of being, doing, and seeing the world with a common objective of doing it together as a team, unit, or partner.

GOD WANTS US TO COLLABORATE WITH HIM

God does not need us to pair with Him; He wants us to collaborate with Him. Think about it in this way; if you are in a relationship and the other person tells you they need you, it is all about them and very little about you. When someone says they want you, they are acknowledging that you have something of value to add. They are letting you know that you are important. At that point, it is no longer about them and what they want, instead, it is about you and what you bring to the process. This is a sign that they value what you have, and they want to be a part of you sharing yourself with them and others. This is what God is saying to us. He wants us, He definitely doesn't need us in our broken, sinful state. He wants us for who He made us to be, not what we have become. He wants to partner with broken you, so He can introduce you to the whole you.

God wants us to collaborate with Him, along with His Son, Jesus, and the followers of the faith message. Therefore, before getting too deep into this, I want to remind you that God calls you by name. He knows who you are. He knows everything about you. He knows your strengths and weaknesses. He called you. He chose you to be His partner in whatever area you have been bestowed. God is big enough to collaborate with the whole world and still have room for more. He can give us more than we can receive, so your call is not a mistake.

THE ENEMY OF PROGRESS IS STAGNATION

The enemy of progress is stagnation; the enemy of faith is playing it safe. The good news is, you are not alone, nor do you have to do it alone. Many are called but few are chosen. You have been called and you are chosen. If you accept His partnership, success is assured if you stay the course. The road will not be easy, but at the end of the journey, you win, if you refuse to faint or quit.

If you want to make it in this world, you need some partners to come alongside you and do what you cannot. The word *partnership* is one of those words we hear all the time and think we understand. We don't really understand partnership the way we should.

One of the definitions of partner is to share. It is no longer in use in our modern language today, but if we use it for just a moment, we can begin to understand more of what we are being asked to do or asked to accept. God is asking us if He can share His love of people with His people through, and by, His people. It is sad that we want to relinquish such beauty so we can keep the worthless ashes of our pride. We want to take all the credit. We want to be able to say, "I did it my way."

Let us apply this in a practical way. What qualities do we need to look for in an individual to ensure they are up for the task of partnership on a mission, vision, or cause? Each mission requires a certain set of skills to accomplish the task with the least amount of wasted energy. For example, **you can use a stapler to fasten your shirt, but a button, zipper, or snaps are more efficient.** When doing anything, we should consider the purpose, time, and resources needed to complete the task. We can use whatever we want to do whatever job, but we must always ask, "Is this the best tool for the job?"

Ask Questions

When you pick a partner, you should ask some questions:

- What do I want to accomplish?
- How much time will it require to accomplish this task?
- What resources can I access to accomplish this task?
- Does this task need to be broken down into even smaller parts?
- How many parts and how much time for each part will the task require?

- What are the mile markers for each part as well as the whole task?

- How will we gauge success?

Once you have taken an inventory and assessed what you have and need, look for those who can come alongside you to complete the task.

- Whom do I know that is able to do these tasks?

- Whom do I know that is willing to do these tasks?

- Who do I know that would be excited about doing these tasks?

- What would it cost to get this person?

- What information do I need to provide them with to get them onboard?

- How will we split the work?

- How will we split the reward?

- What does this person bring that can make completing the mission more efficient, beyond the skill to complete the task?

- Who will carry the risk?

- Can I get along with this person for the long haul?

As you can see, there are many questions we need to ask to complete a simple task. The more complex the task, the more questions that must be answered, and the greater number of people required to complete the task in a timely manner. We must get the right person involved in the right position at the right time with the right motivation. This approach can make the most daunting task seem like child's play. The issue then is that most of us don't have the time nor do we want to go through the Q & A required to make a great choice. We will usually settle for a good choice.

The Difference With Jesus

Let us go back to the offer that is on the table by God the Father and His only begotten Son, Jesus the Christ. Whom did Jesus pick for His great commission? Jesus chose a tax collector, an angler, a thief, a tent maker, and a doctor. They all had one thing in common; they were the right persons for the job that Jesus needed done.

Let us look at Judas. He was a thief. He was known to steal, yet, Jesus called him to be one of His. Jesus even called him friend after he betrayed Him. Why would Jesus call him a friend and he betrayed Him?

We want to change people and then we become angry when they show us that they are who they said they were. Do not pick them because they look the part; pick them because they are the part. We often take what looks like something to us and throw away the most valuable thing. We are visual people. We like what looks good on the outside, on paper. We will go along with them because they look the part. We don't need a partner who looks good only, we need one who is good.

A partner is a person who is active and engaged in a vision, purpose, or task with another person or group of individuals. The role of any partner is to complete the vision or, at the very least, move it along toward completion.

AN EFFECTIVE PARTNER

Are you collaborating with someone who is not active and engaged in the purpose and the process? Are you that person who people connect to, but you are not engaged, active, or committed to the purpose, vision, or task?

A partner is someone who carries the load when you are not able to, as well as carry the load with you. To be an affective partner, we must be able to help lift the load when the people we are with cannot carry the load any longer. Jesus was such a partner. He took the load when we could not.

A true partnership is one hundred percent you and one hundred percent them. You cannot expect to give little of yourself and expect your partners to give one hundred percent of themselves. A partnership that is unbalanced is a partnership that is destined to fail. If you are not true to yourself, you can never be true to anyone else.

A healthy partnership requires effort and if you and your partners are not one hundred percent committed to the vision, both of you are wasting each other's time. When Jesus asked the man if he would be made whole, if the man had answered no, he would not have been healed. Jesus was asking the man to partner with Him in his own healing by exercising his faith. (*See John 5:6-9*)

There must be a commitment from all partners, not just one. How long would a marriage last if one is committed and the other is not? We must be willing to let go of the false and grab a hold to the real. Hold on to the real thing and let go of what looks good but is not good.

Partnering is an act of humbling oneself, to let someone else share in the glory as well as the load. There are people waiting to help us get to our goal. All we need to do is not be afraid to ask for help.

Life is too short to wait to make a change. We must learn to change early and often so we can cultivate a habit of being adaptable. Seek first the Kingdom of God and His ways of doing and being, then HE will add all things. *All things* include partners, finances, space, time, ideas; whatever is needed to complete the task will be provided when you collaborate with Jesus first, and seek to know how the kingdom operates.

Be sure to guard your tongue, or you will give life to your death, instead of breathing life into your purpose. Partner with

God and trust Him to provide the rest. Let the Holy Spirit be your guide.

Chapter 7 Outro

How beautiful a love to have in God the Father that He would give His only begotten Son to us and then share His Son's wealth with us. God is asking us to partner with Him to save a sinful, sick and dying world.

The God of all creation is asking us to be His partners through Christ Jesus. What a wonderful partner to have; the Creator of it all. If you partner with Jesus, remember that God the Father is and always desires to be the CEO, COO and CFO, not because He has an ego like man, but because He knows the plans He has for man. Will you partner with God the Father in your life?

Chapter 7 Take Away

1. **We need to partner with the right people** at the right time for the completion of a goal/vision, with the right collaborates, i.e., the Holy Spirit and Jesus, who are our direct connection to God the Father.

2. **We have a great start for living** a life of purpose and success, but we require more partners.

3. **We have all this technology to help us stay connected**, but we suffer from a lack of a real connection. We are

lonely in a world full of people who we cannot connect to. Let's stop trying to connect and just connect.

4. **God is big enough to collaborate** with the whole world and still have room for more. He can give us more than we can receive, so your call is not a mistake.

5. **A true partnership is one hundred percent you and one hundred percent them.** You cannot expect to give little of yourself and expect your partners to give one hundred percent of themselves. A partnership that is unbalanced is a partnership that is destined to fail.

CHAPTER 8

Leadership: Learning to Follow, So We Can Lead

Get ready as we set sail for the ride of your life, where truth is tested, friendships are forged, and partnerships emerge. As you journey through life, you will have to board another Ship; the Ship called Leader. Be prepared, for this Ship is a bumpy ride. The waves are always warring when this Ship sets sail. This Ship is not for the faint of heart. It is to test you and bless you for all you have learned along the way. It is aboard this Ship that you become like our prototype Jesus. If you are willing, you can become the chief servant. This Ship will teach you what it means to lay down your life for someone else. John C. Maxwell, bestselling author and motivational speaker, wrote: *"A leader is one who knows the way, goes the way, and shows the way."*

What does it mean to be a leader? A true leader is likened to a noble king, one who oversees the welfare, well-being, and development of those under his leadership. A good king, like a good leader, is graded on how well his followers are doing under his leadership. Modern day leaders think leadership is about them. They want to be served, not serve. As a leader, one must be the chief servant. You must be willing to go without, so they can have. You give your best, so they can have the best. Leadership is not a role one should take lightly. When someone trust you enough to follow your guidance, please be sure to often check your GPS (GIVING, PRAYER, and SUBMISSION). Where are you in relation to Gods' purpose for you as a leader?

GPS Defined

Giving - How much time are you giving to the Father so you can hear correctly and accurately what to do and when to do it? Timing is critical to success.

Prayer - How often are you seeking the Father for information on matters other than spiritual? When you lose your way, you may want to ask Him which way from there. Ask this question often, *"What can I do to be better at any given task?"*

Submission - How well do you submit to leaders above you, those who HE sent to help you develop? How well do you submit to the Father's will when it is in direct conflict with your own?

Nahchon D. Guyton

BECAUSE PEOPLE FOLLOW THEM, DOESN'T MAKE THEM A LEADER

We seem to live in a society that glorifies self-service, selfishness, and doing it alone. If you ask anyone who made it to the top of any ladder, and they are honest, they will tell you someone helped them along the way. A good leader is one who helps others along the way. A good leader is going to invest in his people and know what they need to do to get the best results. John Joseph Powell wrote, *"It is an absolute human certainty that no one can know his own beauty or perceive a sense of his own worth until it has been reflected back to him in the mirror of another loving, caring human being."*

Many of us have followed someone at some point for different reasons. We follow people who look like they know where they are going. However, just because people follow them, doesn't make them a leader. It just means one is in front and some people are following behind. A leader is responsible to do and be the best they can be, because they understand the importance of the role of leader. A true leader knows they will be the first to go without, the first to take the hit, and they will not pass the blame.

Leaders must make sure they can handle the responsibility along with the pressure that comes from such a position. Most people would crack under such pressure because they are unprepared to deal with the weight of true leadership.

WHY WERE THEY ABLE TO ACHIEVE SUCH GREATNESS?

Now the whole earth had one language and one speech. And it came to pass, as they journeyed from the east, that they found a plain in the land of Shinar, and they dwelt there. Then they said to one another, "Come, let us make bricks and bake them thoroughly." They had brick for stone, and they had asphalt for mortar. And they said, "Come, let us build ourselves a city, and a tower whose top is in the heavens; let us make a name for ourselves, lest we be scattered abroad over the face of the whole earth." But the Lord came down to see the city and the tower which the sons of men had built. And the Lord said, "Indeed the people are one and they all have one language, and this is what they begin to do; now nothing that they propose to do will be withheld from them." (Genesis 11:1-6).

What traits should we develop or look for in a good leader? If you were in a leadership position, what traits would you want to develop to be better equipped for your job?

We are individuals who come together for a common goal. In the above passage, we see the power of coming together for a common goal. Notice what the scriptures says, *"indeed the people are one."* That is what great leadership can do; it can bring people together in such a way that they become one in language, heart, and action.

When we come together for a common purpose in unity, the supernatural will meet the natural.

> *For where two or three are gathered together in My name, I am there in the midst of them. (Matthew 18:20)*

God is telling us that if we want real power we must come together with other liked minded believers.

Why were those at the Tower of Babel able to achieve such greatness that it got the attention of God, the Creator, resulting in Him coming down to confuse their language? It was the power of unity. People who are gathered together with a single purpose can move Heaven and Earth. The people at the Tower got God's attention because they had a single vision, a single heart and a single speech. God knows what He put in us, and if we come together with a single focus, there are no limits to what we can accomplish.

Once we get a singleness of purpose, we will attract other like-minded people. We must be clear on our single purpose so we can develop singleness of heart and speech in the community.

An undeveloped, unlearned, unfocused, undisciplined or selfish person will make a poor leader. Leadership is about serving, not being served. If you are in leadership because you want your way, then you are in the wrong role.

My Grandmother used to say, *"Who told you this was all about you? Wait your turn!"* In other words, what makes me think I am that important that I can bypass others? She was telling me to get my mind off myself. If I am thinking about myself, I would miss the bigger picture.

You cannot give or receive with a closed hand. In both situations, your hands must be open. This applies to your heart and mind as well. You cannot lead or be led with a closed heart. You must be open to receive from someone, give to someone and walk alongside someone. This is what I believe:

> *Life is not fair, so do not look for it to be. Life is not fair. If it were fair, we would be food for the animals and not the other way around. Fair would be stopping a person as soon as they made a mistake, so they never had a chance to hurt anyone else. However, this is not how life is; life is merciful, just, but never fair. We must move past the mindset that something needs to be fair when it comes to life. You should be fair, but you should not expect life to be fair. God set life up on a system of balance, which is full of mercy and grace. If life were fair, there would be no second chances.*

Be the leader that you want to follow. If you don't want to be that person, then be like the example set before us in Jesus Christ. No matter what you decide, decide to be an example, because whether you know it or not, someone is watching you and some of them will do what you do, and say what you say. Change the future by changing the way you live today.

Story Of A Good King

The story of Jesus is God coming in the form of man to experience life as us, so He could guide us in living a life in victory. He was able to influence people to action on behalf of others. He was able to influence twelve men to go out and away from their families and friends to help others by spreading the Gospel. Jesus' influence was so impactful that today we are still moved by His teachings and doing what He requested of those twelve men.

If we are to lead, we must understand a few things about who we are and where we have influence. We cannot be a leader to everyone, but we can be an influence to most people we encounter by the way we carry ourselves.

Before It All, He Was

Before the galaxies and the universe came into existence, HE was. Prior to earth's formation, the stars covering the sky, and the oceans covering a third of the earth, HE was. Before the sun graced the heavens and shed its light on the Earth, HE was. Before time was set in place as a bookmark in eternity, HE was. Before you or me, HE was. He went before it all to make a way for us to follow. HE was, is, and will always be before it all. He is the Leader of all leaders; the One to honor above all human accomplishment. He is the true King. He shed His blood that we may have a way back to the throne of grace. He gave up the ghost so, in earthly vessels, the Comforter would be left to guide us into all knowledge and all truth. All we need to do is say yes to our new heavenly Guest and play host.

He was before our grief, torment, and pain. He was before our good days and our bad. He was before it all. Therefore, when something shows up that we are not familiar with, on Him we can call. He went before us, so He could bring us through. He is before it all, so when times get tough, on our knees we should fall, and on His name, with prayer and thanksgiving, we should call. 'Jesus' is all we need to say. He did it all. He wrote the Book, set the map, made the plans for the life we could live and opened the way. We are not alone. He left us a Comforter, a Friend, and a Counselor. He left His Spirit to give us hope, bring us hope and show hope.

Do not fear the day nor the hours that come with their troubles. Before it all, He was, so trust Him. Does He not have all power? Of course He has all power. There is nothing made that He did not make. He is the beginning and the end, the Alpha and Omega, in Him we move and have our being. When you think of it that way, what is a car note, electric bill, cancer, or job loss, if we follow the one true Leader who has proven He is good and faithful?

We will encounter many issues, but we have to trust, believe, and rest in Him knowing that He has shown us repeatedly that He is faithful and so good. We need to stop being like stiff-necked children who rarely do what we should, taking the heartache, pain, and disappointments so we can do it our way. Disobedience comes with a price to pay; the grave.

The grave could not hold Him, and hell could not keep Him. He was before Satan fell from grace. He was before it all. Upon His name we must call. He is a Leader who is also a friend.

WHAT HAVE YOU BEEN SAYING?

We say more through our actions than we could ever say with mere words. Our gestures, facial micro expressions, posture, and the tone of our speech will say much to the hearer about what we are saying prior to one word leaving our lips. We say much without speaking an audible word.

What have you been calling into your realm by your actions? Whom are you called to influence? All these are questions you must answer, if you want to walk as an influential leader. Jesus asked Peter, *"Who do they say that I am?"* Peter answered. Then Jesus asked him, *"Who do you say that I am?"* It was a question of great importance for the purpose God, the Father, had in mind for Peter. It was also important for Jesus to hear the answer Peter would give. You need to be able to answer the same questions Jesus asked Peter, if you want the fullness of your purpose on this planet. Who do you say Jesus is in your life? Jim Rohn writes, *"The challenge of leadership is to be strong, but not rude; be kind, but not weak; be bold, but not a bully; be thoughtful, but not lazy; be humble, but not timid; be proud, but not arrogant; have humor, but without folly."*

Modern Leader

Jesus is a great Leader but what makes a great modern leader? Most leaders lead based on how they see themselves and not how others see them. Some leaders lead men into war and victories; some lead men into service and helping the world's poor and needy. One example of a great modern leader is one who leads from where they are. They use their position, resource and time to influence, promote and demonstrate positive change in their immediate surroundings. He understands how others view him and he leads with that understanding, so he can influence those who follow.

Self-Perception

Consider this Jewish story as an illustration of self-perception. There was once a prince who lived with his father and mother, the king and queen, in a splendid fashion. He received the finest education and upbringing. To his parents' chagrin, one day the prince went through an identity crisis and concluded that he was really a turkey and not a human being. Initially, the king and queen thought he was kidding. However, after he stopped joining them at the royal table and instead, moved under the table and sat there naked and pecking at crumbs, they knew that serious trouble was afoot.

The prince's strange behavior caused indescribable angst for his loving parents, and intense embarrassment for the royal family at large. The king was ready to spare no expense for the person who could cure his son. The finest doctors and psychiatrists of the land came and tried to cure the prince, all to no avail. The king was at a loss, until a gentle-looking wise man came to the palace.

"I hereby offer to cure the prince free of charge," declared the man. "My only condition is that no one interferes with anything I do."

Intrigued and desperate, the king and queen readily agreed. The following day, the prince had company under the table. It was the wise man.

"What are you doing here?" asked the turkey prince.

"Why are you here?" countered the man.

"I am a turkey," responded the prince emphatically.

"Well, I am also a turkey," the man replied. With that, he began to gobble like a turkey and peck at the crumbs on the floor. The prince was convinced.

A few days passed, then one morning, the wise man signaled to the king to bring him a shirt. He said to the prince, "I do not see any reason a turkey can't wear a shirt." The prince thought about it and agreed, and soon the two of them were wearing shirts.

Soon the wise man asked to be brought a pair of pants. He said to the prince, "Is it forbidden for turkeys to wear pants?

Certainly not!" The prince thought it over and agreed, and soon the two of them were wearing pants. So, the process continued. Shortly thereafter, the wise man convinced the turkey prince that it was not forbidden for turkeys to eat human food, which was surely tastier. Then came sitting at the table and enjoying human conversation. Within a short time, the turkey prince, although still maintaining that he was a turkey, began conducting himself exactly like a regular person.[2]

Fortunately, most of us do not suffer from turkey complexes. But here is a question we can all ask ourselves: *Am I limiting my potential because of my self-perception?*

A Good Leader

John Quincy Adams wrote, *"If your actions inspire others to dream more, learn more, do more and become more, you are a leader.*

There are some commonly agreed upon qualities that makes for an overall great leader. Great leaders are rarely known when they are in the role of leadership. Their true value is often seen after they have stepped down or moved on to another role. It is only then that it becomes clear what the individual left behind.

---

[2]

http://www.chabad.org/library/article_cdo/aid/612171/jewish/The-Chicken-Prince.htm

Arnold H. Glasow says, *"A good leader takes a little more than his share of the blame, a little less than his share of the credit."*

To be a good leader, one must be willing to take the blame. Leadership comes with a high boiling point so most leaders are in the proverbial hot water more than they let on to those who they are leading. Some people in leadership do not take this part of the process well, so they are hard on everyone and look for someone to blame. It is not good leadership to blame the very people you are called to serve.

If a person did cause an issue, a good leader will provide a safe enough environment for such a person to not be ridiculed and judged. Jesus was willing and did take the punishment that was due all of us. He stood in the gap and took the beating, the ridicule, and the crucifixion of the cross that we may have life. A good leader will take the blame for their team.

Jesus took the blame, but He did not become a doormat. He became a servant who was willing to train His people so they could become worthy of such a sacrifice. Today, so-called leaders seek to be served. They forget the meaning of true leadership, as set by the living example of Jesus.

To Lead Is A Gift

A leader should never ask a follower to do something that he himself is not willing to do. God asked Abram to sacrifice his only son because He knew He was going to sacrifice Jesus for our sakes. Jesus never ask us to do what He has not done. I am using Jesus as the leadership model for several reasons, the main reason being that He is the only leader I know who died, rose again, and was able to tell us how to defeat death.

Leadership is more about serving others than having others serve us. Today, many have moved far away from what it means to lead. To lead means you go first, you take the hits so those who follow do not have to. A good leader makes a way when there is no way, so those who follow can see the path clearly.

Leadership is not a glorious task, as we like to make it out to be, but it is one of honor and privilege. To lead is a gift. Anyone who follows you must first give you the gift of trust. Can we find such leaders today? These leaders are a rare breed.

Jesus had a heart for the people, and the vision (business) as well. He allowed Himself to die so He could lead the people to a better life. A great leader will often sacrifice their comfort to feed the vision (business) as well as the people. Great leaders do not sacrifice their people for their comfort, nor will they sacrifice the vision (business) either. They find solutions to do both, even if they must suffer for a while.

> *My brethren, let not many of you become teachers, knowing that we shall receive a stricter judgment. (James 3:1).*

A teacher is a leader. Their role is to train the people in the ways of God. It is expected that whatever you teach, you must be great at it, or at least good at it. Many people are great teachers, but not great doers themselves. This does not diminish the truth in what they are saying but, for some, it does just that. People lose credibility because they have not done what they are teaching.

EXPERIENCE TRUMPS THEORY EVERYTIME

Many people can accurately tell someone else how to do something, but they cannot do it for themselves. To be a leader in some arenas, for example, leading a team or a squad of warriors, we must be in the front and we must have influence. We can also lead from behind because leading by influence allows us to lead from any position in the organization. As an influencer, we will have an effect on the group, as well as the named leadership. This amount of influence is what makes us a leader. If we are not the named leader, we must influence to build and accomplish the dream. An influence leader should not use their influence to tear down and cause strife. Nevertheless, because we are in front does not mean we are ruler or king, it just means we are a chief servant. Remember, no matter where you fall in the ranks, if you have influence, you can and should lead with the heart of a servant and not a tyrant.

HOW ARE YOU AT FOLLOWING?

I can tell what type of leader you will be by how well you serve others. Your lead-ship is an expression of your heart. No person is capable of judging or seeing the intents of a person's heart, but we can see the fruit of the heart.

Our heart will always tell its position by what it values. Our heart will tell the truth about us, even if our lips lie and refuse to form the words of truth. Our fruits are the results of what our heart values. In our heart, we could be seeking acceptance, position, or honor, or to be counted among them that have done something great. Whatever the reason, it has everything to do with the "me" and nothing to do with serving, so you are not ready to lead because you are not willing to be honorable in serving as you follow.

Leaders grow through trials, failures, and tribulations. It is a shame that we only want to show the Facebook part of life; the good parts and never the bad. We never want to share our hurts, doubts, and failures with others, even with the knowledge that it may just help them be better.

The Bible is clear in calling those who compare themselves among themselves fools. Don't compare yourselves to one another, but rather share yourselves; your true self. By sharing your true self, you will grow and allow others to grow as well. We should honor leadership, but not in the way of idol worship or putting them on a pedestal. We honor by being respectful, helping and serving where we can to move the vision forward. No matter where we are, we have the opportunity to demonstrate true leadership.

OPPORTUNITY TO DEMONSTRATE LEADERSHIP

We call sports figures leaders. We call actors and television personalities leaders. Some of them truly are leaders, but most of them are not. We call them leaders because they are in the spotlight or because they won some award. Being at the top of your game is a sacrifice. It takes hard work, long hours and commitment to be a world class athlete, performer or top earning actor. There is always a cost to being a leader. Leading is self-sacrificing, not self-gratification. I agree with Israelmore Ayivor who said, *"Contrary to popular opinion, leadership is not a reserved position for a particular group of people who were elected or appointed, ordained or enthroned. Leadership is self-made, self-retained, self-inculcated and then exposed through a faithful, sincere and exemplary life."*

Woodrow Wilson also said, *"You are not here merely to make a living. You are here in order to enable the world to live more amply, with greater vision, with a finer spirit of hope and achievement. You are here to enrich the world, and you impoverish yourself, if you forget the errand."*

From the above quotes you can see what leadership is about. It is centered on what you can give, not what you can take. If you are to lead well, you must learn how to serve well. You learn to serve by following or you will never rise above your own selfishness. There are numerous cases of people rising to the top and self-destructing or falling from grace. The reason for this is that their talent, skill, or ability was able to get them there, but their heart, integrity, or character could not keep them there. They never learned how to serve, so the weight of being there was too much for their character to bear, so they imploded, fell from grace or even committed suicide.

Leaders are fashioned through survival, learning, and sharing. They go through storms and can tell you about it. Leaders are forged by going through the fires of life and living to tell their story. I am not saying we need to have a great tragedy or grow up on the bottom side of popular society to become a great leader. We all face challenges with a can do and will do attitude and this is what makes a great leader. We will not be an effective leader if it is always our way or the highway. That attitude may get some traction at first, but in the end, it will create broken allegiance, dishonor, discord and anger in the ranks. Johann Wolfgang Von Goethe aptly says, *"Treat people as if they were what they ought to be, and you help them become what they are capable of being."*

HEART OF A GOOD LEADER

A leader will not always be what we want them to be. Good leaders will not be perfect. We should not look for perfection, but look for a heart to learn, willingness to admit errors, and the character to correct those errors. If they are willing to learn, they are able to lead, if they are humble enough to serve and not look to be served. Leadership is an honor, not a right. If we ever have the honor to hold people's trust as a leader, we must do the best and be the best we can. We cannot have a hard heart, if we expect to be a great leader.

The Bible provides us with so many examples of great leaders, average leaders, and poor leaders.

> *This is a faithful saying: If a man desires the position of a bishop, he desires a good work. A bishop then must be blameless, the husband of one wife, temperate, sober-minded, of good behavior, hospitable, able to teach; not given to wine, not violent, not greedy for money, but gentle, not quarrelsome, not covetous; one who rules his own house well, having his children in submission with all reverence (for if a man does not know how to rule his own house, how will he take care of the church of God?); not a novice, lest being puffed up with pride he fall into the same condemnation as the devil. Moreover he must have a good testimony among those who are outside, lest he fall into reproach and the snare of the devil. (1 Timothy 3:1-7)*

Let us break down each of these verses to see how they point to leadership in modern times.

> *This is a faithful saying: If a man desires the position of a bishop, he desires a good work. (1 Timothy 3:1).*

On the surface, this is a straightforward verse, but it makes a point worth pointing out; it is a good thing to aspire to lead people into the truth. This gives leaders the ability to share with others.

I do believe there are people who are born with the gift to influence others. These people have followers, and they usually don't know where they are going or why people are following them. People who do not know or understand the purpose of something will abuse it. This is true for men and women who do not understand their purpose and end up living a life of abuse. They suffer abuse or they abuse others.

TRAITS OF A LEADER

> *A bishop then must be blameless, the husband of one wife, temperate, sober-minded, of good behavior, hospitable, able to teach. (1 Timothy 3:2).*

Let's take the word *bishop* and replace it with *leader*. A leader must be blameless. You are not to be the type of person who does wrong. You are blameless. You seek to do right for people and by people. You are a person of integrity in respect to your wedding vows. You are loyal, faithful and not into multiple spouses, which was a common practice in the day this was written. You are a vigilant person who is watchful and alert, especially when it comes to avoiding danger.

As leaders, we are to protect and prevent harm to those in our care. We need to be sober, not given to excessive behaviors and practices. We should not be addicted to food or drink, but exercise moderation in all things. We are apt to teach because we have a tendency toward sharing information in such a manner that people can easily grasp or learn the material presented.

> *Not given to wine, not violent, not greedy for money, but gentle, not quarrelsome, not covetous. (1 Timothy 3:3).*

"Not given to wine" is an old term that is not used much today. We now call such a person an alcoholic; someone who is addicted to wine or strong drink. This is not saying we should not drink wine but be temperate and in control at all times. We should be patient; able to endure trials calmly or without complaint. We need to stay the course, despite opposition, difficulties or adversity and be willing and able to bear the weight of time.

We should not be a covetous person who is overly consumed with a desire for wealth and possessions, especially as it relates to someone else's possessions.

> *One who rules his own house well, having his children in submission with all reverence. (1 Timothy 3:4).*

This verse does not condone or support dictatorship in the home, as some would interpret it to mean. This verse is about a husband/father being highly respected in his home by his wife and children. The goal is not to create a spirit of fear in the home but to ensure everything is in its proper place to make sure the home runs well. We are admonished to serve God with all our heart and mind, and to ensure that our children are well behaved and respectful. *Do you have what it takes?* Without Jesus, the answer is no. I have a history that supports my answer. I have made choices and decisions without Jesus that was catastrophic. I am not able to be a great leader, or anything else, without Him. With Jesus, I can do all things.

> *(For if a man does not know how to rule his own house, how will he take care of the church of God?). Not a novice, lest being puffed up with pride he fall into the same condemnation as the devil. (1 Timothy 3:5-6).*

How can we hope to take care of God's house (Earth and people), if we cannot or will not take care of our own? How can we lead God's people, if we cannot lead our family and ourselves? The Bible speaks of this as it pertains to a man, but all of these apply to both men and women.

The next part of the verse is very important because we must have a place to practice. The one who has never been in a role of this magnitude, or a similar role, is not ready to be a leader.

Are you able to manage the little you have been given? If not, why would you look for more? The position of a leader can get one puffed up and filled with pride, resulting in you falling into condemnation. Going after something you want without being tested to see if you can endure it could lead to your death. Don't just want something for the sake of saying you have it. Think long and hard about why you want it. This applies to leadership and all other areas in your life.

Leadership is not a job, but a calling. Being a Bishop is not a position to take lightly. Timothy is informing us to be cautious of pursuing leadership and to be prepared to undergo scrutiny and pressure. You are in an unfit role if you have never served anyone. If you don't know how to lead yourself, how can you lead God's people?

> *Moreover he must have a good testimony among those who are outside, lest he fall into reproach and the snare of the devil. (1 Timothy 3:7).*

This is my favorite part of the text. We must be a person of good reputation with people who are not part of our inner circle and those who are less fortunate than we are. To me, this is the heart of a great leader.

Jesus endured so that we could experience redemption from the pain and suffering that did not benefit Him in any way. Yet, He endured the pain of the cross for the people who were to come, that they may have life and have it more abundantly.

DESIRE TO SERVE

If you want to be a great leader, you must be willing to commit to the process of growth, development, and learning. There must be a willingness to follow the great examples first, if you ever hope to become a great leader. You will never be your best, if you do it alone. Very often, you will have to leave some people behind; those who are not ready to grow, change or be better, so when they are ready, you can be in a position to help and eventually pull them forward toward the mark that God set for them. God has a place for them where they have access to grace, mercy and love to continue onward. You must be willing to pull them and not push. A leader must be someone who draws people to them, not one who pushes them towards something. Leaders are servers. If you desire to lead, then you must ask yourself this question, *"Do I desire to serve?"*

We are all on ONE JOURNEY. We call that journey life. We all have one life to live. Things happen "As The World Turns." God called us to be His "Guiding Light" for "The Young and the Restless." He calls "All My Children" so we can live like the "Bold and the Beautiful." You are not alone on this journey. He provided us a body of believers called the church, which is a "General Hospital." You can isolate yourself, but that is not the goal of the Father. He gave us 7 Ships (***Relationship, Friendship, Discipleship, Stewardship, Partnership, and Leadership)*** that we can grab hold of to take us through this journey we call life.

God invested His life in you so that you may have a life to live. Live your life, considering His investment. Your life is not your own, it has been bought with a price. He gave up His life for us so let us not be so self-seeking that we forget that. We are called to be a light to the lost and dying world. Let your light shine bright; let your purpose be clear and your heart open to hear the voice of the Lord calling you into a greater role, greater than you could ever imagine. You are called to leadership; you are called to servanthood.

To be great in the kingdom, we must be the chief servant. Above that, there is no higher honor. Live your calling with a pure heart, the mind of Christ and the will of God being done in, though, and around you. Live as Christ lived; live on and with purpose.

Chapter 8 Outro

No matter where you are in life, you are a leader. You may not feel like a leader, or you may be a poor leader, but one thing is true; we all have influence in some area of life. How we use that influence will determine what kind of leader we are.

Leadership is not about having your way; it is about serving your way to help others grow and succeed. It's easy to dictate, but it takes a real leader to serve.

Chapter 8 Take Away

1. **When someone trust you enough to follow your guidance**, please be sure to often check your GPS (GIVING, PRAYER, and SUBMISSION). Where are you in relation to God's purpose for you as a leader?

2. **The story of Jesus is God coming in the form of man** to experience life as us, so He could guide us in living a life in victory.

3. **A leader should never ask a follower** to do something that he himself is not willing to do.

4. **Leaders are fashioned through survival, learning, and sharing.** They go through storms and can tell you

about it. Leaders are forged by going through the fires of life and living to tell their story.

CHAPTER 9

Who Am I? The Age-Old Question

I wanted to include a chapter on identity since most of us fail to fulfill our purpose because we fail at knowing who we are and to Whom we belong. We are not carbon copies of anyone, but a mosaic called self with bits and pieces from everyone we have encountered, every book we have read, every sight we have seen, along with everything we have experienced since the day we came into the earth. Our goal is to move from copying someone else into looking and being more like Christ Jesus. We can easily mimic others and this allows us to learn early on, but at some point, we must move beyond imitation and press forward to our full, authentic selves.

WHO AM I?

There are a million answers to this question. One answer is that we are the summation of the thoughts we think and the choices and decisions we make based on our exposure and experiences.

REAL POWER VERSUS PERCEIVED

You are not those self-defeating thoughts that sprout up out of nowhere. Your past has nothing to do with tomorrow. You are the thoughts you choose to think consciously and subconsciously. You can make today bad and tomorrow worse, and it all depends on what you choose to think. I know ideas and thoughts come that are so far from who you are that you easily dismiss them. Then there are those thoughts that are so close to home that you wear them like a badge of honor.

You are in control of your thought life. You are the pilot of the plane. Your thoughts are the wings and your tongue is the control stick. You are the one in real control. I can point a gun at your head and tell you to eat, drink, and be merry. This is perceived control or power because I am creating a mental painting, a picture of power. This picture is based on fact because a gun is a powerful weapon. Even though I have perceived power and control, I still cannot make you eat, drink, and be merry. I could force the food in your mouth and use my hand to move your mouth to simulate chewing. But no matter what I do or say, you have the power to refuse my demands. You are the one with the real power.

In every area of your life, you are in control. You have real power; others only have perceived power. If you comply with their demands, it is because you have been deceived to think they have real power, or you are afraid of what they will do if you don't comply. Never confuse perceived power with actual power.

A mirror can only reflect your outer part, but the outer part of anything is only the beginning. The real depth is hidden beneath the surface. The wealth of a person is not in what they possess but in what they do with what they have. You can be the best version of yourself or the worse by choice. Your value is not in your imitation of others but in the originality of you being your authentic self. You are the captain of your ship called choice. You are always in control of them and no one can take your choices, but you can give them away by not being active in making choices.

BEYOND THE PASSIVE AND INTO THE ACTIVE

To know who you are will require you to move beyond the passive and into the active. You must actively seek to know yourself better each day, just as you seek to know the Father God better each day. The only way for you to know who you are is to know who He is. You will need to spend time with the Creator, if you want to know your full potential. How do you get to know someone? By spending time with them, studying them through listening to their ideas, and watching them to see if their actions match up to their words. God watches over His word to perform it; do you? If not, you are a hypocrite and your word is worthless.

How do you classify yourself? How would others view you? Are you a person of integrity? Do you do what you say? Do you work to keep your word? Are you mindful of not agreeing quickly since you understand the value of keeping your word?

You are priceless, original, peculiar and worth the wealth of the world; you just don't know it. Until you know it, you will only exist and not live. The reason for our existence is not a destination, but a life-long journey. Every day you should learn something new about yourself. Allow today to be the beginning of that journey. Make today the beginning of something great. Let today be your "re-do"; your fresh start. Let this be where you decide to choose to be the best version of yourself. That is part of the course of living on this side of eternity. Even feeling guilty is a choice. You must decide here and now how you are going to live. Are you going to wallow in self-pity and defeat from the past, or are you going to take hold of the reins and live today as if it was your last, without fear, shame, and condemnation? Are you going to get up, dust yourself off, say to yourself that you are better than this and admit that you have been living beneath your privilege and do something different, not later but right now?

The first thing you may want to do is repent and ask God to be the head of your life. Give your cares over to Him because He cares for you. Let Him take the wheel. Let Him lead you into a better version of yourself. Nothing you have been through will catch Him off guard. He will not be surprised at how dark some of your days have become. He gave up His life of plenty, in exchange for your life of lack.

Are you willing to let go of this little life, and take hold of a bigger more abundant life by letting Him take control of every aspect of your world? I must warn you; this mission, if you choose to accept it, will change the course of your life and the lives of all who come after you. This is not a mission for the fearful and self-seeking. This is mission possible for them who believe. Do you believe that God is and that He is a rewarder of them who diligently seek Him? If you answered yes, then you are well on your way to discovering who you are and to Whom you belong. In all that you gain along the way, make sure you get an understanding of what it is He is calling you to do. Today is the day that you become a better version of yourself.

The Race For Life

In a land far away, but as close as this moment, was a town filled with people. Some would say that the town was overpopulated. The town was called Dynitikós. Little did they know that Dynitikós would expand and no matter how many people came, it would never reach its full capacity. Every month of every year there was a race. Some of the town folks would say it was a death race.

The desire to live free and be more was so strong that despite the danger of failure and death, every month of every year the people of Dynitikós would forge forward. No one can remember the day the race started. The town legend says the first Dynitikósioan began to look for a way out of town and found it and he created and left a map to Skopós. He wanted to make sure that anyone who was courageous and determined and who had the faith and desire to go would know the way, so he mapped it, marked the route, and left instructions with road signs pointing the way. As the legend goes, he was not heard from again, so the town's people believed he reached Skopós; and died fulfilled in the new land. After that day, all who saw the map set-off to reach the new land. This is the legend of the race for life in Dynitikós.

Dynitikós is where the race for life was held and all could participate. The reward was a trip to Skopós; a new land where they would be able to let out what lay deep within their hearts. The reward was so appealing that everyone joined the race.

In a small corner of Dynitikós lived Eseís. He had no father, and no mother either that he could recall. Dynitikós was somewhat a crowed place and everyone looked the same; their individual distinction buried deep within. The only way to release it was to leave Dynitikós and race so they could meet Efkairía. Everyone yearned for the moment when they would be able to release their hidden ideas, talents, and reach fulfillment.

Eseís decided to participate in the race. Eseís was not discouraged but determined to win. Prior to the start of the race, Eseís started to feel anxious, pressed, and under a great deal of pressure. He pushed forward with an immeasurable amount of force.

Eseís felt like the odds were so great that failure was closer than victory. Eseís said within, *"Despite all the challenges and the delays that may come against me, I will run my race and finish."* Eseís was one of the last ones to get out of the starting gate, but he was determined. He was ready to run his race and win. As he ran, a million more people came behind Eseís, pushing up against him. Eseís decided that he was not going to give in or give up. His inner determination would not let him dwell on any thought too long. Eseís prepared himself, setting his eyes on the goal. Eseís said to himself, *"I will use this pressure to propel me forward."* He did not know how, but he was sure the people pushing behind him would help.

Eseís ran, not looking to his left or to his right, he just ran. He ran his race and after three or four hours of running, which felt like days, he could see the first milestone. He knew only one could survive and he was determined to reach the first milestone. Eseís was not aware, but another person had come alongside him with determination to reach the milestone as well.

The race became extremely dangerous because only one could make it through. Eseís was persistent and pressed with all he had, and he made it through. Eseís was victorious. There was a sign in place that read "Avgo." Eseís rushed in and rested while the staff of the Avgo catered to him. It had been about eight days since Eseís began the race. Eseís found a bed in the corner of the Avgo and just rested.

Eseís started having visions. Eseís was in a near catatonic dream state, unaware he was being placed on a boat and pushed out to sea. When Eseís awoke, he remembered crossing over and through the first milestone. Eseís recalled taking a nap at Avgo; the nap did Eseís well.

The next day, Eseís fell into a dark hole. Eseís was feeling concerned that the victory was not a victory but a trap, as if someone played a cruel trick. At that moment, the thought came to mind that the reward was pain, or some weird science experiment, as his body began to change into something other than what he knew to be him. Over the next several months, he began to grow strange appendages from every part of his body. Eseís thought that he had been running for nothing. Why would they allow such a cruel race to occur with false promises and misguided hope?

Most participants died before ever reaching the finish line. He heard this voice inside of him, but outside at the same time. The voice was faint, almost sounding distant. Eseís thought it was strange. Eseís thought again that the race was all a ploy against him and the people in his town. The voice came back, *"Now, now! It's okay."* Eseís began to feel calmer, but he was still thinking about the race.

Eseís was recalling some of the signs he encountered along the course, *"It's not over til it's over."* One of the other signs posted along the way read, *"The race for life is not a sprint."* Another sign read, *"10-month marathon with little to no breaks in the process."* The final sign he saw read, *"The Life Race motto: Always press forward, always move forward, if you turn to look back, you can and will die."*

Eseís thought about that last sign for a long time. He allowed that sign to motivate him to keep moving forward, never looking back, just pressing toward the mark, thinking to himself, *"I must finish what I started. I must finish the race."*

About four months had passed, Eseís looked around and saw a door at the far end of the corridor. He ran towards it. Eseís became more determined to get to the other side, so he pushed with all he had, and the door gave way.

Eseís called out to see who was there with him and no one answered. Eseís was starting to feel alone. Someone or something was maneuvering an object onto him. It felt like a vacuum, something that provided a constant flow of fluids. In the same moment, he was placed on another boat. Eseís felt pushed, controlled, and lost. Eseís' experience was leaving him feeling an endless emptiness in the middle of nowhere. He remembered the sign, *"Always press forward, always move forward, if you turn to look back, you can and will die."* He felt trapped. Eseís, was feeling anxious, hungry and afraid.

Every day, Eseís was challenged with new discoveries. Before he could even think about where he was and how he was going to finish the race, he was whisked away by a strong wind. The wind pushed his boat to land, and he found himself on a beach. Eseís looked at the foods and began to taste, finding his preference. Once he realized what he liked, he searched for those particular foods.

Several days and months passed since Eseís landed on the beach named Epoasi. While on the island of Epoasi, Eseís lost all sense of time. He grew comfortable. Eseís settled in and began to eat and sleep, eating so much, he outgrew the island. The feeling of being closed in and cramped began to develop. Eseís could move, but not as freely as before. The new world had become a lot smaller since he first landed.

He heard voices increasingly in the distance. He was uncertain, but one of the voices was oddly familiar. He settled down to take his normal nap and heard many voices in the surroundings. There was a pressure against him, but he could not see anyone. Eseís began to grow rapidly. Not knowing what to do, Eseís, just thought about the motto, *"Always press forward, always move forward, if you turn back you can and will die."* It had been several weeks since he last saw the island.

The sky started to collapse around him. He was pressed on every side. The sky burst and the sea that brought him to the island of Epoasi rushed away. There was no more sea, no more island, just a little bubble remained. Eseís, in that bubble, was just floating. As the bubble contracted around him, he heard the motto in his mind, *"Always press forward, always move forward, if you turn back you can and will die."* Eseís said, *"I will get there."* Eseís started pushing his hands and legs to stretch the bubble. He needed more room. He pushed and kicked trying to make more room for himself but to no avail; the bubble grew smaller.

Suddenly, there was darkness and more pressure from all sides. Eseís saw a pinhole size light at the end of a long dark tunnel. Eseís turned, twisted and tried to get into a position where he could reach the light. An ease engulfed him as he heard the voice from the island, the one that brought him comfort. Unexpectedly, there was a sharp smack on his backside and Eseís let out a scream. Eseís was passed around from strange creature to strange creature; poked and prodded. Finally, he was given to the creature with the calming voice. Eseís could now fulfill all his potential, if he did not quit.

MORAL OF THE STORY

Dynitikós is the Greek word for *potential*. **Skopós** is the Greek word for *purpose*. **Efkairía** is the Greek word for *opportunity*.

We all start our race for life filled with potential, and we must constantly move and grow to fulfill that potential. There will be uncomfortable positions as we explore our potential, but if we continue, we will reach the promise land of a new life. We should never grow comfortable in any position of the race. We started the race for life by being the fastest and most determined. To fulfill our potential, we must keep that determination. Progress forward, whether great or small, is still progress.

I returned and saw under the sun that—the race is not to the swift, nor the battle to the strong, nor bread to the wise, nor riches to men of understanding, nor favor to men of skill; but time and chance happen to them all. (Ecclesiastes 9:11).

You ran well. Who hindered you from obeying the truth? (Galatians 5:7).

I could wish that those who trouble you would even cut themselves off! For you, brethren, have been called to liberty; only do not use liberty as an opportunity for the flesh, but through love serve one another. (Galatians 5:12-13).

Therefore we also, since we are surrounded by so great a cloud of witnesses, let us lay aside every weight, and the sin which so easily ensnares us, and let us run with endurance the race that is set before us, looking unto Jesus, the author and finisher of our faith, who for the joy that was set before Him endured the cross, despising the shame, and has sat down at the right hand of the throne of God. (Hebrews 12:1-2).

Closing Remarks

You have only one life, a chance that is filled with many choices so you can fulfill your purpose.

> *I call heaven and earth as witnesses today against you, that I have set before you life and death, blessing and cursing; therefore choose life, that both you and your descendants may live; that you may love the Lord your God, that you may obey His voice, and that you may cling to Him, for He is your life and the length of your days; and that you may dwell in the land which the Lord swore to your fathers, to Abraham, Isaac, and Jacob, to give them. (Deuteronomy 30:19-20).*

Do not allow the enemy of purpose to come steal, kill and destroy your hope for a better life. Jesus is that hope. God is more than able to provide us hope, but we must accept the gift. You are capable of more; to do, give, learn, and share more. You must be willing to let Jesus be your prototype. Jesus made you to be victorious in Him. Without Him, you can do nothing. It makes no sense to live beneath your privilege, to struggle, when you don't have to.

Life is full of trials, tribulations, and difficulties. I am not suggesting that once you find your identity in Christ Jesus that your life will be gardens filled with roses, or whatever your favorite flower may be. Quite the contrary, in fact, your life could become much harder. Even my worst day with Him is better than my best day without Him.

Decide now to let Jesus be the head of your life. If our eyes never meet and our hands never touch, know that for your success, I will pray. I see you as a fellow traveler who Jesus loves so much that He gave His life that you may live and have life more abundantly. What an honor and a gift it is to be called a child of God; to be called His friend. Until then, move forward, and press in to Jesus.

This Is Just The Beginning.

Until Next Time!

APPENDIX

QUESTION AND ANSWERS

These are some questions I have asked myself or someone asked me in the past. I felt it right to give an answer for them here.

Do real men cry?

Yes, Jesus wept.

> *Then the Jews who were with her in the house, and comforting her, when they saw that Mary rose up quickly and went out, followed her, saying, "She is going to the tomb to weep there." Then, when Mary came where Jesus was, and saw Him, she fell down at His feet, saying to Him, "Lord, if You had been here, my brother would not have died." Therefore, when Jesus saw her weeping, and the Jews who came with her weeping, He groaned in the spirit and was troubled. And He said, "Where have you laid him?" They said to Him, "Lord, come and see." Jesus wept. Then the Jews said, "See how He loved him!" (John 11:31-36).*

Jesus was not crying because Lazarus was dead. He knew what He was about to do. He was not weeping because He was taken off guard or surprised at the news. He was weeping because His heart was filled with compassion for the people who were there mourning the death of a dear friend and brother. Jesus was fully aware of the death of His friend.

> *These things He said, and after that He said to them, "Our friend Lazarus sleeps, but I go that I may wake him up." (John 11:11).*

This was Jesus fulfilling the scriptures found in Romans 12:15, *"Rejoice with those who rejoice, and weep with those who weep."* Jesus was also feeling the pain of His friend's death and the sadness of the family. He was showing compassion for the family and their pain and grief. We need to be more like this as we deal with hurting people in our midst.

What is love?

Love of both God and man is fundamental for a true relationship as it pertains to the Father through Christ Jesus, whether as expressed in the Old or the New Testament.

Love is first and foremost a gift. Love is not something that one falls into, it is something that one chooses to share. Love is a gift given to us and given from us. We can show love and not know the history of the person we are sharing our love with. Often, we get love confused with emotions. Love is not an emotion. Love is what makes us move. Love gives us life and so much more. Love sustains us. Love is why we are. Jesus declared, *"On these two commandments hang all the Law and the Prophets."* (See Matthew 22:40 and Mark 12:28-34).

> *Love suffers long and is kind; love does not envy; love does not parade itself, is not puffed up; does not behave rudely, does not seek its own, is not provoked, thinks no evil; does not rejoice in iniquity, but rejoices in the truth; bears all things, believes all things, hopes all things, endures all things. Love never fails. But whether there are prophecies, they will fail; whether there are tongues, they will cease; whether there is knowledge, it will vanish away. For we know in part and we prophesy in part. (1 Corinthians 13:4-9)*

The word love and charity are interchangeable because love is an action word as well as a choice, similar to charity.

TYPES OF LOVE FROM THE GREEK

What are the types of love?

The Greeks had different names for Love:

"EROS" OR EROTIC LOVE, this is carnal or fleshy love. It is most exhibited when self loses control in pursuit of physical encounters; lust. An immature belief of love; the thought is purely carnal, shaped around a shortsighted view of sexual fulfillment; passion.

"PHILIA" OR AFFECTIONATE LOVE, friendship. The second type of love the ancient Greeks valued is philia which is far above Eros because it is a love between equals. Applied to us, the love felt for a dear friend; male or female, this love has nothing to do with the physical. A love that is a respect for another person developed through enduring a common event together thus, admiration for the other person grows. You have love for a teammate; coach of your squad, sorority, fraternity and members of your small groups at church. You have a closeness to them and feel loyal to them.

"STORGE" OR FAMILIAR LOVE. Although storge closely resembles philia in that it is a love without physical attraction, storge is primarily kinship and familiarity. This is the love you feel for your parents, sisters, brothers, and close friends no matter how bad they are. You feel protective and close to them because they are your family; they are your kin. There is an old saying, *"Blood is thicker than water."* I take that to mean some will often side with family and close friends over good judgement.

"LUDUS" OR PLAYFUL LOVE. Although ludus has a bit of the erotic eros in it, it is much more than that. The Greeks thought of ludus as a playful form of love, for example, the affection between young lovers. This is young love; it is heart palpitations, flirting the childlike innocence we face opening our hearts to the newness of love, and a new relationship. Playfulness in love is an essential ingredient that is often lost in long-term relationships. Yet playfulness is one of the secrets to keeping the childlike innocence of love alive, interesting, and exciting.

"MANIA" OR OBSESSIVE LOVE is a type of love that leads a partner into a type of madness and or obsessiveness. It occurs when there is an imbalance between eros and ludus. This is where the person is "in love" with the idea of "being in love." This is where the person has made the feeling the prize and person the object. They have lost sight of reality and are holding on to the idea.

"PRAGMA" OR ENDURING LOVE is a love that has aged, matured, and developed over time. It is beyond the physical. It has transcended the casual, and a unique harmony has formed over time. It is "PHILAUTIA" OR SELF LOVE. The Greeks understood that to care for others, we must first learn to care for ourselves. This form of self-love is not unhealthy vanity nor self-obsession that is on personal fame, gain and fortune, as is the case with Narcissism.

"AGAPE" OR SELFLESS LOVE is the highest and most radical type of love according to the Greeks. Agape is selfless, unconditional love. God the Father has given this love to all of creation. Jesus gave it on the cross when HE gave His life to redeem us back to the Father. Loving in this manner goes beyond anything that we would consider rational. Agape is to love a person despite what they have done. This is what everyone should strive for; unconditional love.

LOVE

Why should one show love?

The greatest gift we can give anyone is our time and attention and it is called love. We should take our time, which is a limited commodity on this side of the spiritual realm, and spend it helping someone else become better. Jesus mandated us to love our enemies as our self.

How does one love their enemies?

To love someone who is not worthy of love, in our eyes, is a sacrifice. We need to look at them as Christ did; He loved them so much that He gave His life that they might live. We need to show them that love. We are to demonstrate that commitment to them so they can see and experience Jesus in us. To love the unlovable is not something you can do without Christ. You must let the love of Christ fill your heart and mind and give you His vision for that person. Until then, one will not be able to love their enemies.

How do you give love to another person?

You share yourself, talents, and gifts with someone and expect nothing in return. You help them, without expectation; no strings attached. God requires us to share His love with the world. We are to show His love and grace to all humanity.

> *A new commandment I give to you, that you love one another; as I have loved you, that you also love one another. (John 13:34).*

This is not a suggestion but a command. We are to show everyone we meet Christ's love. In Matthew 5:43-46, we see Jesus telling the people that it has been said, "Love them who love you." He corrects that tradition and cultural understanding and states what it means to give love.

> *But I say to you, love your enemies, bless those who curse you, do good to those who hate you, and pray for those who spitefully use you and persecute you, that you may be sons of your Father in heaven; for He makes His sun rise on the evil and on the good, and sends rain on the just and on the unjust. For if you love those who love you, what reward have you? Do not even the tax collectors do the same? (Matthew 5:44-46)*

He ends by asking them a question. I will paraphrase, *"What is the benefit in such a short-sighted approach; to only give and show love to them who love you?"* He is giving us another command that we must love those who come against us.

If you want to get back at someone, the best revenge is to love them.

> *Therefore, "If your enemy is hungry, feed him; if he is thirsty, give him a drink; for in so doing you will heap coals of fire on his head." (Romans 12:20).*

How is Jesus the same as God the Father?

The Father has always been. He was not created. He is love. He is a Spirit.

> *God is Spirit, and those who worship Him must worship in spirit and truth. (John 4:24).*

Jesus is the body that the Father created so that He may come to earth and die that we may all have an opportunity to be restored back to Himself.

Jesus is also the Word of God. Everything that is, Jesus made it. Jesus was born into the world for the purpose of redemption and reconciliation.

> *For it pleased the Father that in Him all the fullness should dwell, and by Him to reconcile all things to Himself, by Him, whether things on earth or things in heaven, having made peace through the blood of His cross. And you, who once were alienated and enemies in your mind by wicked works, yet now He has reconciled in the body of His flesh through death, to present you holy, and blameless, and above reproach in His sight— (Colossians 1:19-22).*

What does it mean to put my flesh to death?

To answer this properly, we must first become aware of the fruits of the flesh. Galatian 5:19-21 provides us with a list of the works of the flesh; and the fruits of the flesh. I am going to list them here, with modern definitions. It should become clearer that what we show in our flesh is carnal in nature.

> *Now the works of the flesh are evident, which are: adultery, fornication, uncleanness, lewdness, idolatry, sorcery, hatred, contentions, jealousies, outbursts of wrath, selfish ambitions, dissensions, heresies, envy, murders, drunkenness, revelries, and the like; of which I tell you beforehand, just as I also told you in time past, that those who practice such things will not inherit the kingdom of God. (Galatians 5:19-21).*

FRUITS OF THE FLESH

Adultery, Fornication, Uncleanness, Lasciviousness, Idolatry, Witchcraft, Hatred, Variance, Emulations, Wrath, Strife, Seditions, Heresies, Envying, Murder, Drunkenness, Reveling, and such the like.

FRUITS OF THE FLESH DEFINED

As I was studying this list, I found some of these definitions hard to handle. Some are so common to humankind's make-up that I found it hard to swallow. Therefore, I know we all fall short of God's grace and we all need to be saved from ourselves.

Please note: all definitions are from the Webster Dictionary1828, not the Merriam Webster.

Adultery

Violation of the marriage bed; a crime, or a civil injury, which introduces, or may introduce, into a family, a spurious offspring. In common usage, adultery means the unfaithfulness of any married person to the marriage bed.

In a scriptural sense, all manner of lewdness or unchastity, as in the seventh commandment. Adultery of the heart, consisting of inordinate and unclean affections. No unclean person hath any inheritance in the kingdom of Christ and of God.

Fornicate

To commit lewdness, as an unmarried man or woman, or as a married man with an unmarried woman.

Lewdness

The unlawful indulgence of lust; fornication, or adultery.

Uncleanness

Not clean; foul, dirty, filthy. Foul with sin. That holy place where no unclean thing shall enter. Not in covenant with God. Lewd; unchaste.

Lasciviousness

Looseness; irregular indulgence of animal desires; wantonness; lustfulness. Tendency to excite lust and promote irregular indulgences.

Idolatry

The worship of idols, images, or anything made by hands, or which is not God. Idolatry is of two kinds; the worship of images, statues, pictures made by hands; and the worship of the heavenly bodies, the sun, moon, and stars, or of demons, angels, men, and animals.

Excessive attachment or veneration for anything, or that which borders on adoration.

Witchcraft

The practices of witches; sorcery; enchantments; intercourse with the devil.

Hatred

Great dislike or aversion; hate; enmity. Hatred is an aversion to evil, and may spring from utter disapprobation, as the hatred of vice or meanness; or it may spring from offenses or injuries done by fellow men, or from envy or jealousy, in which case it is usually accompanied with malevolence or malignity. Extreme hatred is abhorrence or detestation.

Variance

Difference that produces dispute or controversy; disagreement; dissension; discord. A mere variance may become a war. Without a spirit of condescension, there will be an everlasting variance.

Emulations

The act of attempting to equal or excel in qualities or actions; rivalry; desire of superiority, attended with effort to attain to it, generally, in a good sense, or an attempt to equal or excel others in that which is praise-worthy, without the desire of depressing others.

In a bad sense, a striving to equal or do more than others to obtain carnal favors or honors.

Wrath

Violent anger; vehement exasperation; indignation; the effects of anger; Gods wrath, in Scripture, is His holy and just indignation against sin.

Strife

Exertion or contention for superiority; contest of emulation, either by intellectual or physical efforts. Strife may be carried on between students or between mechanics. Contention in anger or enmity; contest; struggle for victory; quarrel or war. Opposition; contrariety; contrast.

Seditions

The sense of this word is the contrary of that which is naturally deducible from sedo, or sedeo, denoting a rising or raging, rather than an appeasing. Nevertheless, to set is really to throw down, to drive, and sedition may be a setting or rushing together.

A factious commotion of the people, a tumultuous assembly of men rising in opposition to law or the administration of justice, and in disturbance of the public peace. Sedition is a rising or commotion of less extent than an insurrection, and both are less than rebellion; but some kinds of sedition, in Great Britain, amount to high treason. In general, sedition is a local or limited insurrection in opposition to civil authority, as mutiny is to military.

Heresies

From a Greek word signifying (1) a choice, (2) the opinion chosen, and (3) the sect holding the opinion. In the Acts of the Apostles it denotes a sect, without reference to its character. Elsewhere, however, in the New Testament it has a different meaning attached to it. Paul ranks "heresies" with crimes and seditions (Galatians 5:20). This word also denotes divisions or schisms in the church (1 Corinthians 11:19). A "heretical person" is one who follows his own self-willed "questions," and who is to be avoided. Heresies thus came to signify self-chosen doctrines not emanating from God (2 Peter 2:1).[3].

Envying

To feel uneasiness, mortification, or discontent at the sight of superior excellence, reputation or happiness enjoyed by another; to repine at another's prosperity; to fret or grieve one's

---

[3] www.biblestudytools.com

self at the real or supposed superiority of another, and to hate him on that account. Pain, uneasiness, mortification or discontent excited by the sight of another's superiority or success, accompanied with some degree of hatred or malignity, and often or usually with a desire or an effort to depreciate the person, and with pleasure in seeing him depressed. Envy springs from pride, ambition, or love; mortified that another has obtained what one has a strong desire to possess.

Murder

The act of unlawfully killing a human being with premeditated malice by a person of sound mind. To constitute murder in law, a person killing another must be of sound mind or in possession of his reason, and the act done with malice pretense, aforethought or premeditated; but malice may be implied, as well as expressed. To kill a human being with premeditated malice is murder.

Drunkenness

Intoxicated; inebriated with strong liquor. Proceeding from intoxication.

Reveling

To feast with loose and clamorous merriment; to carouse; to act the bacchanalian. A feast with loose and noisy jollity. Some men ruin the fabric of their bodies by incessant revels.

Because I listed the works of the flesh, I thought it would only be fair to list the fruits of the Spirit with their definitions.

There is hope. We don't have to take this journey of life alone. We have a Helper, the Holy Spirit, along with an example of how to do it.

FRUITS OF THE SPIRIT

Love, Joy, Peace, Longsuffering, Gentleness, Goodness, Faith, Meekness, Temperance.

FRUITS OF THE SPIRIT DEFINED

Love

In a general sense, to be pleased with; to regard with affection, on account of some qualities which excite pleasing sensations or desire of gratification. In short, we love whatever gives us pleasure and delight, whether animal or intellectual; and if our hearts are right, we love God above all things, as the sum of all excellence and all the attributes which can communicate happiness to intelligent beings. To have benevolence or good will for.

Joy

The passion or emotion excited by the acquisition or expectation of good; that excitement of pleasurable feelings which is caused by success, good fortune, the gratification of desire or some good possessed, or by a rational prospect of possessing what we love or desire; gladness; exultation; exhilaration of spirits. Joy is a delight of the mind, from the consideration of the present or assured approaching possession of good. To rejoice; to be glad; to exult.

Peace

It is a state of quiet or tranquility; freedom from disturbance or agitation; applicable to society, to individuals, or to the temper of the mind.

Longsuffering

Bearing injuries or provocation for a long time; patient; not easily provoked.

Gentleness

Dignity of birth. Softness of manners; mildness of temper; sweetness of disposition; meekness.

Goodness

The state of being good; the physical qualities which constitute value, excellence, or perfection; kindness; benevolence; benignity of heart; but more generally, acts of kindness; charity; humanity exercised.

Faith

To trust; to persuade, to draw towards anything, to conciliate; to believe, to obey. Belief; the assent of the mind to the truth of what is declared by another, resting on his authority and veracity, without other evidence; the judgment that what another state or testifies is the truth.

Evangelical, justifying, or saving faith, is the agreement of the mind to the truth of divine revelation on the authority of God's testimony accompanied with a pleasant acceptance of the will or esteem of the heart; an absolute trust in God's character and declarations in the doctrine of Christ. This being with an unreserved surrender of the will to his guidance and dependence on His merits for salvation. In other words, that firm belief of God's testimony, and of the truth of the gospel, which influences the will, and leads to an entire reliance on Christ for salvation.

Meekness

Softness of temper; mildness; gentleness; forbearance under injuries and provocations. In an evangelical sense, humility; resignation; submission to the divine will, without murmuring or peevishness; opposed to pride, arrogance, and refractoriness.

Temperance

Moderation; particularly habitual moderation regarding the indulgence of the natural appetites and passions; restrained or moderate indulgence; as temperance in eating and drinking; temperance in the indulgence of joy or mirth. Temperance in eating and drinking is opposed to gluttony and drunkenness, and in other indulgences, to excess.

www.ingramcontent.com/pod-product-compliance
Lightning Source LLC
Chambersburg PA
CBHW071328110526
44591CB00010B/1064